Migration Law in the United States

Migration Law in the United States

Second Edition

Maria Isabel Medina

This book was originally published as a monograph in the International Encyclopaedia of Laws/Migration Law.

Founding Editor: Roger Blanpain
General Editor: Frank Hendrickx
Volume Editor: Helen Oosterom-Staples

Wolters Kluwer

Published by:
Kluwer Law International B.V.
PO Box 316
2400 AH Alphen aan den Rijn
The Netherlands
E-mail: international-sales@wolterskluwer.com
Website: lrus.wolterskluwer.com

Sold and distributed by:
Wolters Kluwer Legal & Regulatory U.S.
7201 McKinney Circle
Frederick, MD 21704
United States of America
Email: customer.service@wolterskluwer.com

ISBN 978-94-035-3340-7

e-Book: ISBN 978-94-035-3341-4
web-PDF: ISBN 978-94-035-3342-1

The Author

Maria Isabel Medina is Ferris Distinguished Professor of Law at Loyola University New Orleans College of Law, LA, United States. She joined the Law Faculty at Loyola after practicing law at Arnold and Porter in Washington, D.C., having served as a law clerk in the U.S. District Court for the Eastern District of Louisiana. She has visited at the University of Athens, Greece, as a Fulbright Scholar, and at Villanova Law School, Tulane Law School and Thomas Jefferson School of Law. She is a graduate of Tulane Law School, where she served as a managing editor of the *Tulane Law Review*. Born in La Habana, Cuba, she earned her Bachelor of Arts degree from Monash University, Melbourne, Australia and a Master of Arts and Master of Fine Arts from the University of New Orleans. She has served as chair of the immigration law section and co-chair of the constitutional law section of the Association of American Law Schools. She teaches and writes in the areas of U.S. Constitutional Law, U.S. Immigration and Citizenship Law, and Gender, Race and Employment Law. She is an elected member of the American Law Institute. She is the recipient of the Loyola University New Orleans 2018 Dux Academicus Award, the highest honor a professor can receive for excellence in teaching and scholarship at her academic institution. Her author page is available at https://ssrn.com/author=395212, and a full list of publications is available at https://law.loyno.edu/academics/faculty-and-staff-directory/m-isabel-medina.

The author thanks Gabriel Silva, Chelsea Rice, Mary Patricia Wray, Todd Feinstein, Allison Griswold and Michael Karam for their assistance with this project.

The Author

Table of Contents

The Author 3

List of Abbreviations 11

Preface 13

General Introduction 17

§1. Immigration History and Statistical Information 17

§2. Overview of National Legal Instruments 33
I. Historical Overview 33
II. Current Applicable Legislation 39

§3. Overview of International Legal Instruments Applicable in the U.S. 45

Part I. Border Control and Entrance 49

Chapter 1. Organization of Border Control 49

Chapter 2. Right to Enter the Country 52

§1. Conditions for Entry: Temporary Visitors for Business or Pleasure 54

§2. Administrative Procedures and Documents for Entry 54

Chapter 3. Refusal of Entry: Inadmissibility 56

Part II. Right of Residence: General Provisions 61

Chapter 1. Short Stay: Nonimmigrants—Visa Waiver Program; B-1 Business Visitors and B-2 Visitors for Pleasure 61

§1. Conditions for Short Stay 61

§2. Administrative Procedures and Documents for Short Stay 61

§3. Legal Position in the Event of Short Stay 62

§4. Position of Family Members 63

Chapter 2. Residence: Nonimmigrants 64

§1. Conditions of Residence 64

§2. Administrative Procedures and Documents for Residence for Nonimmigrants 64

§3. Legal Position of Nonimmigrants 64

§4. Position of Family Members of Nonimmigrants 65

Chapter 3. Long-Term Residence: Immigrants 66

§1. Conditions for Long-Term Right of Residence: Family-Based Admission Categories 66
I. Immediate Relatives of USCs 66
II. First Preference: Unmarried Sons and Daughters of USCs 68
III. Second Preference: Spouses, Children and Unmarried Sons and Daughters of Permanent Resident Aliens 68
IV. Third Preference: Married Sons and Married Daughters of Citizens and Their Spouses and Children 69
V. Fourth Preference: Brothers and Sisters of Citizens and Their Spouses and Children 69

§2. Administrative Procedures and Documents for Long-Term Residence 69

§3. Legal Position of Long-Term Residents: Immigrants 71

§4. Position of Family Members of Long-Term Residents: Immigrants 74

Part III. Right of Residence for Special Categories of Persons 75

Chapter 1. Nationals with Preferential Treatment 75

Chapter 2. Students 76

Chapter 3. Researchers 79

Chapter 4. Labor and Economic Migration 80

§1. Labor Employment 80

§2. Seasonal Workers and Temporary Workers 80

§3. Independent Economic Activities 81

§4. Investment Activities 81

Chapter 5. Humanitarian Reasons 82

§1. Humanitarian Grounds 82

§2. Unaccompanied Minor Children 82

§3. Victims of Trafficking in Human Beings 84

Chapter 6. Asylum 85

§1. Conditions for Admission 85
I. Refugee Status 85
II. Subsidiary Protection Status 88
III. Temporary Protection Status 88
IV. Other: Relief under the Convention Against Torture 89

§2. Procedures 89

§3. Legal Position 90

§4. Position of Family Members 90

Chapter 7. Others: Diversity Immigrants 91

Part IV. Loss of Right of Residence 93

Chapter 1. Conditions under Which the Right of Residence Might Be Lost 95

Chapter 2. Legal and Administrative Procedures 101

Part V. Sanctions 105

Chapter 1. Sanctions 106

§1. Administrative Sanctions 106

§2. Penal Sanctions 106

§3. Detention 108

§4. Expulsion Measures 109

Chapter 2. Sanctions Against Persons Helping Illegal Immigrants or Residents 112

§1. Human Smuggling 112

§2. Human Trafficking 113

Part VI. Legal Remedies and Procedural Safeguards 115

Chapter 1. Legal Remedies in Case of Refusal of Right to Enter, Stay or Reside 115

Chapter 2. Procedural Safeguards 120

Part VII. Access to the Labor Market 123

Chapter 1. Overview of Applicable Legislation 123

Chapter 2. Conditions for Entitlement to Work in the Country as an Employed Person 125

§1. General Conditions 125

§2. Administrative Rules and Procedures 127

§3. Conditions for Special Categories of Workers 128

Chapter 3. Sanctions Against Irregular Participation in the Labor Market 129

§1. Sanctions Against Employers 129

§2. Sanctions Against Workers 130

Chapter 4. Legal Remedies and Procedural Safeguards 131

Preface

United States (U.S.) migration operates in a system that is remarkably open, transparent and, for the most part, generous and favorable toward migration. This perspective perhaps reflects its origins, which, as discussed below, were diverse from the start, and its development, which was similarly diverse both as a result of sizable territorial growth, such as with the Louisiana Purchase, the acquisition of the southwest and northwest regions, present-day Alaska, and the Hawaiian Islands, and also because throughout its history it has continued to interest and accept a substantial number of immigrants from different cultures, ideologies, religions, races and countries. Despite the general acceptance and commitment to immigrants and diversity, the U.S., paradoxically, has also witnessed and tolerated considerable hostility to most immigrant groups, including the Chinese, the Irish, the Italians, the Japanese, and Mexicans. This duality is perhaps inescapable in a country the size and diversity of the U.S.

The 2016 presidential election reflected this duality toward immigrants and immigration as polarized and clashing political views, rather than the more nuanced and complicated national dialogue that had prevailed in prior decades. The election of President Donald Trump resulted in a number of presidential initiatives all directed at changing U.S. immigration policy and practice dramatically. Within weeks of entering office, President Trump had issued a series of executive orders prioritizing the completion of a wall along the U.S.-Mexico border, pledging to detain and deport even more resident noncitizens than under the previous administration, targeting cities and states that opted not to collaborate in apprehension and removal of undocumented persons, and suspended admissions of noncitizens including refugees from seven Muslim countries. In addition, the Trump administration effected changes in the administration and law dealing with asylum, including expanding the use of expedited process in removing persons who request asylum and refusing admission to persons who request asylum for full consideration of their claims. The original executive orders and subsequent policy initiatives led to political and litigation challenges.

As this manuscript was in production, the United States elected Joseph R. Biden, Jr. as its new president. The Biden administration has signaled abandonment, rescission, or reconsideration of many of his predecessor's policy changes. The Biden administration has abandoned the policy of forcing asylum seekers at the southern border to remain in Mexico, the suspension on admission or entry of noncitizens from Muslim countries, and the diversion of federal funds to construct the wall at the U.S.-Mexico border. In addition, the new administration has announced a new prioritization for enforcement and removal of noncitizens, refocusing efforts on persons who are removable because of criminal convictions. In particular, the Biden administration has proposed new legislation to provide a path to permanent residence for many irregular migrants. U.S. immigration law, therefore, is in transition; the ultimate fate of many of the Trump administration rules has not yet been determined.

U.S. immigration law is primarily found in federal statutes and federal regulations. A number of federal agencies described in this monograph are charged with implementing these statutes. These agencies make available on their websites a considerable amount of information about immigration law and processes. American immigration law is complicated and, for this reason, it may be difficult for lawyers and non-lawyers to accurately understand and navigate immigration process through public websites. Nonetheless, most scholars will find a wealth of information made available by the U.S. government on the web.

The U.S. Constitution does not expressly provide an affirmative grant of power to the federal government to regulate immigration. However, the Constitution recognized that Congress had power to regulate importation of persons into the U.S., principally by restricting Congress from banning the international slave trade until 1808, in the Migration clause of Article 1, section 9 of the Constitution. Early U.S. Supreme Court cases recognized that as a sovereign nation, the U.S. had plenary power to control its territory; thus, the U.S. could control entry into the U.S., and removal of noncitizens. Moreover, the Supreme Court reasoned, other clauses in the U.S. Constitution, like the power to provide rules for naturalization and to regulate interstate and foreign commerce, made it clear that the power to regulate immigration is necessary and proper to effectuating other express powers granted to Congress. Courts treat the power to regulate immigration as plenary with Congress and the executive; thus, states generally lack the power to regulate in this area, unless authorized by Congress. Increasingly, the modern Congress has opted to authorize states to collaborate or play a more active role in enforcement of immigration law. Notwithstanding, some Constitutional protections and limits apply to Congress' exercise of the immigration power and to the states' ability to regulate immigrants as a class, absent Congressional authority. The U.S. Constitution, as interpreted by the U.S. Supreme Court, provides levels of protection for noncitizens in the U.S. and limits the degree of power that federal and state governments may exercise over both citizens and noncitizens in the context of immigration. As a practical matter, the level of protection may be low or minimal, simply because the Supreme Court generally has deferred substantially to Congress and the President in this area. However, the minimal Constitutional guarantee to all persons in the U.S. is one of rationality; the government may not exercise arbitrary and irrational power over persons, and noncitizens in the U.S., generally, are guaranteed protection from irrational or arbitrary abuse of power. To some extent, in nonimmigration related matters, noncitizens in the U.S. enjoy the same Constitutional protections as citizens, except that they remain subject to removal from the U.S. This is an area that is in flux, however, with substantial litigation at the state and federal levels.

As explained above, American immigration law is complicated and represents the interaction of statutes, regulations, federal court decisions, administrative court decisions, Constitutional provisions, executive orders, and agency directives. In the removal context, state criminal law may play a role as well. This monograph presents an overview of American federal migration law, not an exhaustive treatment of the subject. Moreover, American law, in general, and immigration law, in particular, is fluid not static. Courts play a substantial role in interpreting federal statutes, federal regulations and the U.S. Constitution. An essential characteristic of the American legal system is that it tolerates substantial diversity in legal opinion or rules of law. The thirteen federal circuit courts of appeal may often reach different interpretations of federal statutes; the American system allows for, and in fact relies on, these differences in the development of rules of law. Until a particular issue is resolved by a U.S. Supreme Court decision, different rules may apply in different parts of the country. Even after Supreme Court rulings, on matters of statutory law, Congress itself may opt to change the law. Thus, many legal issues or questions in immigration law are not well settled and may be subject to ongoing litigation.

In addition, the administration of immigration law is primarily done by federal agencies headed by federal officials answerable to cabinet-level officers, in turn, answerable to the President. These officials exercise substantial discretion in administering immigration law. Some of their policy directives are not easily or immediately accessible to the public and may be modified by the agency itself in response to legal or practical developments. An example of such an administrative response is the implementation of the National Security Entry-Exit Registration System (NSEERS), a system established in 2002 in response to the September 11, 2001 attacks on the World Trade Center in New York City and the Pentagon in Washington D.C., that required nonimmigrants from twenty-five countries (twenty-four predominantly Arab or Muslim nations in addition to North Korea) to register and report periodically to immigration authorities.[1] The registration program ended in December 2003, and reporting requirements for individuals placed in the NSEERS system upon arrival were minimized but not eliminated. The institution and modifications to the system were all done through federal regulations.

Thus, this overview should not be treated as a definitive legal description of American immigration law, but an introduction to its basic Constitutional, statutory and regulatory structure. The American legal system uses the term "immigration law" rather than "migration law" to describe the legal norms that govern admission into and departure from the U.S., whether for permanent or temporary residence. In addition, the term "immigrant" in the U.S. has a technical meaning under American immigration law, and a secondary meaning, as well, in general American dialogue. Under American immigration law, an immigrant is a noncitizen who does not come within one of the specified nonimmigrant categories; primarily, noncitizens seeking admission to the U.S. for permanent residence. Persons admitted to permanent residence are eligible to become U.S. citizens after five years as permanent residents. American usage, however, also considers immigrants as those citizens who have naturalized. Thus, the word "immigrant" may be used to describe a permanent resident alien or a U.S. citizen who migrated to the U.S. For both the terms "immigration law" and "immigrant," the author conforms to American usage. In the case of the term "immigrant" the term throughout is used to describe permanent resident aliens, unless otherwise specified. Immigration statutes use the term "alien" or

1. 67 Federal Register 52584-01 (2002).

"aliens" throughout. Many scholars, including the author, have criticized the use of the term. Increasingly, U.S. Supreme Court opinions have used the term "noncitizen" rather than "alien," unless quoting or referencing specific provisions in the statutes. The Biden administration's proposed U.S. Citizenship Act of 2021 would amend the immigration statute to substitute the word "noncitizen" for "alien," wherever the term occurs. This monograph uses the term "alien" when it is referencing statutory usage.

Finally, this monograph describes the immigration laws of the U.S. as they operate in normal conditions. The COVID-19 pandemic has brought substantial changes to international travel and the actual operation of migration restrictions, often, has been impacted.

General Introduction

§1. Immigration History and Statistical Information

1. The United States (U.S.) was created as a constitutional republic in 1789 when thirteen states grouped along the north and south-eastern coast of the North American continent ratified the U.S. Constitution. The U.S. first came into being after thirteen colonies declared their independence from Great Britain in 1776. The Treaty of Paris, in 1783, marked the end of the Revolutionary War and formal recognition of the U.S. as an independent state. Until the adoption of the Constitution, the U.S. operated as a confederacy of states. At the time of its creation, the territory was peopled by its native inhabitants, North American Indian tribes or linguistic groups, including the Mohawk, Cherokee, Delaware, Iroquois, Choctaw, Creek, Powhatan, Huron Algonkin, and Shawnee; its native population of European origin, 75% of which were of British origin, another 8% of German origin, and the rest of Dutch, French or Spanish origin; and approximately 500,000 Black slaves coerced to migrate to North America from Africa. In 1790, at the time of the first census, the U.S. recorded a population of approximately 3,227,000.

2. The territory that is now the U.S. contained a number of native tribes, some of whom were eliminated by European, and later, American colonists, and some of whom retain some element of sovereign identity and territorial control under U.S. law. In this monograph, tribes may be identified by tribe names or by linguistic or cultural groupings that may include more than one tribe. Members of Native American tribes are United States citizens (USCs) under federal statutory law and the U.S. Constitution.

3. Parts of what is now the U.S. were settled almost concurrently by the Spanish (Florida in 1565); the English (Virginia in 1607 and Massachusetts in 1620); the French (Mississippi River territory in 1682); and the Dutch (Hudson River in 1624). The Southwestern U.S. was claimed by Spain, and after its independence, Mexico. Indigenous tribes in the south-west included the Lipan Apache, Apache, Comanche, Caddo, Karankawas, Coahuiltecan and Tonkawa in current day Texas; the Hokan, Uto-Aztecan, Chumash, Maidu, Miwok, Modoc, Mohave, Ohlone, Pomo, Shasta, Tongva and Wintu in California; the Anasazi, Folsom, Sandia, Clovis, Cochise, Mogollon, Zuni, Navajo, Apache, Ute, Hopi, and Pueblo in New Mexico; the Nez Perce, Makah, Tsimshian, Coeur d'Alene, Lushootseed in the Oregon Territory (now Oregon, Washington, Idaho and Montana). Non-contiguous parts of the U.S. contained substantial non-White indigenous populations, including in Alaska, the

Aleuts, Alutiiy and Eskimos alongside Russian settlers from at least 1725, until Russia ceded the territory to the U.S. in 1867 and the state was admitted to the Union in 1959. In Hawaii, the original settlers consisted of Polynesian and Tahitian people, joined later by groups of Russians, Portuguese, Spaniards, Germans, Norwegians, Japanese, Koreans and Filipino immigrants, by the time the islands were annexed to the U.S. in 1898 and admitted to statehood in 1959.

4. Early European immigrants migrated for a variety of reasons. Many came for economic opportunity, but some, like the Puritans, Catholics, Quakers, Huguenots and German Pietists, fled religious persecution. Some immigrants, like refugees from the French Revolution, fled political persecution. Some European migrants were coerced: their migration was either a punishment for crime or an alternative sentence for a criminal conviction. Over half of all English and over one-tenth of all Irish immigrants between 1718 and 1775 were convicts. From 1700 to 1775, convicts and prisoners constituted 9% of the total immigrants to the thirteen colonies.

5. Initially, Africans joined European explorers in parts of North and South America as free people. Almost coincidentally, however, European powers, including the Spanish, Portuguese, French, Dutch, and eventually the British, developed a transatlantic slave trade, kidnapping, enslaving and selling large numbers of West Africans in the Americas. In 1619 a group of Africans were brought to the Jamestown colony in Virginia as indentured servants. Indentured servants could gain freedom after finishing their period of indenture. By 1640, however, some Blacks in Virginia were held as de facto slaves and their children inherited the obligation. Between 1640 and 1660, informal Black slavery transformed into Black chattel bondage sanctioned by law. Lifetime servitude was never imposed on Whites in the colonies. By the end of the seventeenth century, slavery had gained legal recognition throughout the British colonies and enslaved Blacks were regarded as human property. Each region passed slave codes to regulate slave activity and to protect White society against slave uprisings. As a result of the international slave trade, the slave population in the English colonies grew from 20,000 in 1700 to 500,000 by the time of the American Revolution in 1776. Most African migration to the colonies, thus, was coerced. The majority of slaves were concentrated in the southern seaboard, in Virginia, South Carolina and Georgia. Only approximately 25% of Whites in the south owned slaves; notwithstanding, the majority of the White population supported slavery as an institution, in part because of the plantation economy and White supremacy ideology, which rendered mere skin color a "badge" of superiority over all other races.

6. The Revolutionary War eroded support for the institution of slavery in the north. In addition to liberal ideas encompassed in the war for independence, memorialized in the Declaration of Independence was a growing abolitionist movement inspired by Quakers, and the marginal importance of slavery to the Northern economy. The revolution itself reflected a divide over slavery and race. The British offered slaves freedom in return for service in their military, yet approximately five thousand free Blacks fought in the war for the new republic. Historian Gary B. Nash described the role of African Americans during the revolutionary period, free and slave, in *The Forgotten Fifth: African Americans in the Age of Revolution* (Cambridge: Harvard University Press, 2006). At the time of the framing of the constitution in 1787, slavery had emerged as a source of division and friction between the new states. Congress, acting under the Articles of Confederation, had banned slavery in the federal territories north of the Ohio River in the Northwest Ordinance of 1787. At the Constitutional Convention, the Framers of the Constitution agreed to compromises that were favorable to the south and the institution of slavery. The original Constitution contains at least three indirect references to slavery: Article 1, section 2 provides that for purposes of congressional apportionment, a slave was to be counted as three-fifths of a person; Article 1, section 9 provided that Congress would take no action concerning the international slave trade until 1808; and Article IV, section 2, clause 3, the fugitive slave clause, ensured the return of runaway slaves to masters. By 1790 there were approximately 700,000 African slaves in the U.S. The division between the north and the south on the issue of slavery widened after adoption of the Constitution. Early abolitionists aimed their efforts at educating northerners about the evils of slavery and the use of law to fight slavery. They relied on a 1772 English case, *Somerset v. Stewart*, involving a writ of habeas corpus filed to test the status of James Somerset, a slave brought into English territory who escaped and asked to be declared a free person. The King's Bench ruled that no person could be forcibly held as a slave in England because no positive law created or recognized slavery in England. During the period between 1780 and 1804, as a result of state legislation and/or court decisions, New England and some middle Atlantic states abolished slavery. Vermont abolished slavery in 1777; New Hampshire and Massachusetts abolished slavery through judicial decision in 1757 and 1783, respectively; Pennsylvania (1780), Rhode Island (1784), Connecticut (1784–1797) New York (1799–1817) and New Jersey (1804) did so gradually. Ohio abolished slavery in 1802; Illinois in 1818 and Indiana in 1816. In 1807 Congress acted to prohibit the international slave trade. Despite the prohibition of the slave trade, there was tremendous growth in the number of slaves in the south. The trade continued to some degree illicitly. In addition, the ban did nothing to slow the domestic slave trade. In 1808, when the international ban went into effect, 1 million slaves resided in the U.S.; by 1830 the number had doubled to 2.1 million. By 1860, poised to fight a civil war over the issue, the number of slaves in the country had risen to almost 4 million.

7. In 1803 the U.S. acquired the Louisiana Territory from France. North American tribes, including the Atakapa, Caddo, Tnica Natchez, Muskhogean and Chitimacha, resided in the Louisiana Territory, followed by French and Spanish explorers and settlers. The territory that became the state of Florida in 1838 was settled by North American tribes, including the Ais, Creek, Timucua, Apalachee, Miccosukee, Yemassee, Calusa and Seminole, and the Spanish, and was eventually ceded to the U.S. by Spain. The Adams-Onis Treaty of 1819 (The Treaty of Amity, Settlement, and Limits between the U.S. and His Catholic Majesty) established the Sabine River as the western boundary between the Louisiana Territory and Spanish-held Mexico. The treaty left most of the southwest to Spain, including California, Texas and New

Mexico (which included Arizona, Nevada, Utah and parts of Wyoming and Colorado) and set the northern boundary of Spanish claims at the forty-two parallel, marking the boundary today between California and the State of Oregon. In 1807 Congress banned the international slave trade and, for the most part, ended forced migration of indigenous Africans into the U.S. But the southern Louisiana Territory, claimed by the French and subsequently, the Spanish, featured African enslaved labor. As parts of the territory sought to join the U.S. as states, whether those states would be admitted as "free" states or as "pro slavery" states became an increasingly contested question.

8. In 1821 Mexico gained independence from Spain and gave Anglo-Americans permission to settle a colony in Mexican territory; by 1836, 35,000 Anglo-Americans had settled in the territory. In 1830 Mexico prohibited further emigration into Texas by settlers from the U.S. Texas settlers rebelled in October 1835 and declared their territory the Republic of Texas. The war with Mexico ended in 1836 when Texas forces defeated Mexican General Santa Ana. In 1845 the U.S. admitted Texas as a state.

9. Military conflicts between the U.S. and Mexico continued over territorial claims in California and concerning the boundary between Texas and Mexico, and war between the two countries broke out in 1846. The Mexican-American War was fought on Mexican territory and culminated in American forces marching on Mexico City. The Treaty of Peace, Friendship, Limits and Settlement with the Republic of Mexico, U.S.-Mex., February 2, 1848, 9 Stat. 922 (Treaty of Guadalupe Hidalgo) marked the end of the war, which resulted in the forced sale of Nueva California to the U.S. for USD 15 million.

10. By 1700, approximately 300,000 Native Americans resided in the California area. Although Spanish, Russian and British explorers laid claim to California, by 1823, the Spanish had established twenty-one missions in New Spain, later known as Nueva California, under Mexico. In 1848 settlers in California discovered gold. The gold rush attracted new migrants to California, including a wave of Chinese workers. California was admitted to the U.S. as a state in 1850. By 1851, 25,000 Chinese worked and resided in the new state. Between 1850 and 1882, the year in which Congress first enacted legislation restricting Chinese migration to the U.S., 300,000 Chinese immigrants had arrived on the Pacific Coast.

11. Between 1820 and 1870, 6.8 million Europeans migrated to the U.S., the majority of them from Ireland (2.7 million) and Germany (2.2 million), many of them Catholic. During this period, it was not uncommon for American companies or American territories to advertise overseas for immigrants. Migration from other areas of the world during this period was dramatically smaller—an additional 700,000 persons from non-European countries migrated to the U.S. This influx of immigrants prompted strong anti-immigrant feelings, particularly against the Irish, and a new political party, the Know Nothings, pushed for restrictions on immigration and for restrictions on states allowing immigrants to vote. In addition, Chinese migration to the Pacific Coast similarly stimulated a push in the west for more restrictive policies on immigration. The addition of new territories, new states and more immigrants to the U.S. had an impact on the slavery debate, as new territories admitted to the U.S. either as slave states or as free states changed the level of support in the federal government for slavery. Shortly after the anti-slavery Republican Party realized the election of Abraham Lincoln as President, southern states began to secede from the Union. Civil war broke out in 1861 when South Carolina state forces attacked Fort Sumter, a federal military fort.

12. Tensions in the U.S. about slavery grew, fueled by dissent over the Louisiana purchase of territory and the south-western territories gained from the war with Mexico. The compromise of 1850 admitted California as a free state, ended the slave trade in the District of Columbia, passed a stronger fugitive slave law, and allowed territories in New Mexico and Utah to decide for themselves whether to allow slavery. This compromise, however, increased tension between north and south. For the south, the end of the slave trade in the District of Columbia suggested that Congress had power to regulate the interstate slave trade. For the north, although California gave the north a majority in the U.S. Senate, allowing Utah and New Mexico to decide for themselves essentially did away with a geographic boundary for the expansion of slavery. Subsequent legislation increased the tensions because it left it to new states whether to come in as a free state or as a slave state. The dispute generated a new political party, the Republican Party, which became the dominant party with the election of Abraham Lincoln. Lincoln became president in March 1861. Shortly after seven states seceded and declared themselves the Confederate States of America. Lincoln's Inaugural Address delivered on March 4, 1861, sought to assure southern states that he would not interfere with slavery within their states. Civil war broke out when Confederate troops attacked Fort Sumter on April 12, 1861. During the Civil War, eleven southern states attempted to secede from the U.S. The war is considered the deadliest war for the U.S. because of the huge loss of American military and civilian life. The war ended on April 9, 1865, when General Robert E. Lee surrendered to General Ulysses S. Grant at Appomattox, Virginia. A few days later, on April 15, 1865, President Lincoln was assassinated.

13. President Lincoln, although unequivocally opposed to slavery, initially did not move to free slaves; instead, his objective was to restore the Union. In 1862, Congress abolished slavery in the District of Columbia, freed runaway slaves and banned slavery in the territories. In September 1862, Lincoln issued the Emancipation Proclamation declaring that all slaves in states still in rebellion on January 1, 1863, would be freed; slaves in the Union and in areas occupied by Union forces, however, were not affected. The Emancipation Proclamation opened the way for enlistment of Blacks in the Union Army. By the war's end, more than 200,000 Blacks were serving in the Army. As of January 11, 1863, 3 million slaves were freed and Black freemen were allowed to serve in the Union army. Some 800,000 slaves were left in bondage and not freed until the adoption of the 13th Amendment in December 1865. In March 1865, Congress passed an act establishing the Freedmen's Bureau to look after refugees and former slaves. The Bureau was authorized to set aside land in the insurrectionary states, up to forty acres of land a year, to freedmen, at an annual rent of up to 6% of the land's value, with an option to purchase at any time.

14. The Civil War led to the adoption of the 13th, 14th and 15th Amendments to the U.S. Constitution. The 13th Amendment, introduced at President Lincoln's request in 1865, prohibited slavery in the U.S. The 15th, adopted in 1870, prohibited discrimination on the basis of race, color or previous condition of servitude on the right to vote. The 14th Amendment, adopted in 1868, defined the status of citizenship under state and federal law and vested U.S. citizenship on the basis of birth in the territory and naturalization; prohibited abridgment of the privileges and immunities of USCs; prohibited states from depriving persons of life, liberty, or property without due process of law; and guaranteed to persons equal protection. The 14th Amendment due process clause has been interpreted by the U.S. Supreme Court to protect persons not just through procedural safeguards but also to protect substantive rights, like the right to vote, the right to privacy, and the right to marry, from state government restrictions. These rights are protected against federal government restrictions by the 5th Amendment due process clause. The Supreme Court has interpreted the 5th Amendment due process clause to guarantee to persons equal protection from federal government restrictions or burdens. Both the equal protection and due process protections apply to persons; thus, immigrants or noncitizens are protected under both clauses. The Civil War and the Reconstruction Amendments (the 13th, 14th, and 15th Amendments to the U.S. Constitution) strengthened the role of the federal government with regards to the enforcement of constitutional rights by giving express power to Congress to enforce the amendments. The amendments enhanced the degree of protection that persons and citizens in the U.S. enjoy from governmental abuse.

15. In 1890 the census reported only 2,637 Japanese in America. Between 1890 and 1900, more than 27,000 Japanese arrived in the U.S. From 1901 to 1910, an additional 58,000 Japanese immigrants arrived. The 1910 census recorded 72,157 Japanese in the U.S.

16. After the Civil War, Congress acted to curtail immigration and, in particular, to curtail immigration from China. In 1875, Congress barred the immigration of women for purposes of prostitution, singling out women from China and Japan, and convicts. Chinese migration to the U.S. resulted from trade relations between the two countries that date back to the earliest years of the Republic. In 1868 the U.S. and China entered into the Burlingame Treaty, amending the Treaty of Tientsin of 1858. The Burlingame Treaty was named after Anson Burlingame, the American Minister to China under the administrations of Presidents Lincoln and Johnson, and the man who led the Chinese mission to the U.S. to negotiate the terms of the treaty. Under the terms of the treaty, both nations agreed to encourage and accept immigrants from each other. Both nations agreed to treat each other's immigrants favorably and to protect their rights while residing in the other country. In addition, the U.S. recognized China's power to control her territory. Although Chinese migration was much smaller in numbers than the Irish and German migration, it generated a demand for more restrictions, particularly after the completion of the transcontinental railroad in 1869 slowed demand for laborers. Particularly on the West Coast, in California, where the majority of the Chinese immigrants resided, public opinion during the 1860s and 1870s clamored for a bar on Chinese migration. At the state level, California enacted a variety of statutory restrictions on the Chinese immigrants, some of which were declared invalid by federal courts. Overall, the American response to the Chinese was not positive and reflected racial and cultural bias. To an extent, some Americans feared that Chinese contract workers were too similar to slave labor; public opinion often thought such workers to be involuntary migrants, part of the "coolie trade." The coolie trade was trade in involuntary workers—workers who had been kidnapped, sold, coerced or misled into being transported to other countries for forced labor. The U.S. prohibited participation in the coolie trade in 1862 during the Civil War. Others were intolerant of the Chinese because of their physical, cultural and religious differences. Moreover, the America-China trade was not as profitable for American companies as had been expected, and China, itself, was not viewed as hospitable to Americans. During much of the nineteenth century, England and China were engaged in hostilities, which to some extent affected relations between China and the U.S.

17. Despite the optimism reflected in the 1868 Burlingame Treaty toward continued migration between both countries, public opinion shifted. In 1880 the Burlingame Treaty was renegotiated with terms that suspended but did not completely prohibit Chinese immigration to the U.S. Under the terms renegotiated in the Angell Treaty of 1880, the U.S. continued to carry the obligation to guarantee protection to Chinese residents of the U.S. In 1882 Congress passed the Chinese Exclusion Act curtailing Chinese immigration to the U.S. for ten years. In addition, the Act obliged Chinese residents to carry a certificate at all times identifying their status in the U.S. Possession of the certificate guaranteed their right to reenter the country after a temporary departure. Subsequently, Congress passed additional statutes further eroding the protection guaranteed to Chinese immigrants under the Burlingame and Angell treaties. The Act of 1888 prohibited the reentry of Chinese into the U.S. after temporary departures. The 1888 Act was challenged by a returning Chinese resident denied reentry into the U.S. The U.S. Supreme Court held in *Chae Chan Ping v. United States*,[2] that the statute properly abrogated the terms of the 1880 treaty and that it was constitutionally valid. Congress went on, in 1892, to renew the Chinese exclusion for another ten years and in 1902 opted to extend the exclusion to the Philippines and Hawaii. The exclusion remained in place until 1943, when China's status as an ally of the U.S. during World War II resulted in more favorable relations between the two countries. American's attitudes toward the Chinese in the early twentieth century continued to reflect racial prejudice and bias. The Chinese were treated similar to Blacks in states where racial segregation norms were enforced. Many cases challenging racial segregation were brought by Chinese plaintiffs.

2. 130 U.S. 581 (1889).

18. The Spanish-American War of 1898, initiated by revolutionary movements in Cuba and the Philippines, resulted in the transfer of control from Spain to the U.S. of Cuba, Puerto Rico, the Philippine Islands, Guam and other islands. Cubans had pursued independence from Spain since 1868. Cubans again issued a formal cry for revolution in 1895. Similarly, in 1896 the Philippine Revolution against Spanish rule began. The U.S. declared war on Spain, when its warship the USS Maine exploded in Havana Harbor in 1898. By the time the U.S. entered the war, both insurgencies had declared independence from Spain. The Treaty of Paris of December 10, 1898, negotiated between Spain and the U.S., without full participation by the revolutionary leaders or governments of Cuba and the Philippine Islands, ended the war. Spain agreed to renounce all rights to Cuba, to cede Puerto Rico and Guam to the U.S. and to sell the Philippine Islands to the U.S. for approximately USD 20 million. The Philippines began an insurrection against the U.S. in 1899 that ended in July 1902 with the capitulation of Filipino soldiers to U.S. forces. The Philippine-American War resulted in the death of thousands of Filipinos and Americans. Although in 1935, the islands were declared a self-governing commonwealth, the U.S. maintained control over the Philippines until World War II when U.S. forces on the Islands surrendered to the Japanese in May 1942. U.S. forces again took control of the islands from the Japanese in 1944 and efforts to declare the Islands independent, initiated in 1935, succeeded in 1946 when the Islands became the independent Republic of the Philippines. The relationship between the Philippines and the U.S., thus, is longstanding and complicated. Understandably, immigration from the Philippines to the U.S. has been strong. Visa backlogs for the family-based preferences for applicants from the Philippines tend to be long.

19. The relationship between the U.S. and Cuba and Puerto Rico is complex and dates back to early European settlements on the islands when Spanish explorers used Cuba and Puerto Rico as bases from which to venture onto the mainland of the North American continent. Later, Puerto Rico and Cuba were involved in the international slave trade with southern states. Today, Puerto Rico is an unincorporated territory of the U.S. with commonwealth status. Puerto Ricans are USCs. Popular movements to change the relationship between Puerto Rico and the U.S. to either statehood or independence have not been successful.

20. Although Spain relinquished control over Cuba and recognized its independence in the Treaty of Paris of 1898, the U.S. failed to recognize Cuba as an independent country and instead placed it under military occupation. In order to secure withdrawal of U.S. occupation forces, Cuba had to agree to the terms of the Platt Amendment. The Platt Amendment restricted Cuba's sovereignty: the Amendment limited Cuba's ability to enter into treaties with other foreign powers; it limited Cuba's power to assume or contract any public debt; it forced Cuba to accept the right of the U.S. to intervene in its affairs; and forced Cuba to sell or lease land to the U.S. Cuba agreed to the terms of the Platt Amendment in 1901. The Platt Amendment remained in force until 1934. While in place, Cuba agreed to lease land at Guantanamo Bay to the U.S. for a military base. The Platt Amendment made it easy for the U.S. to actively intervene in Cuba's political affairs. U.S. forces again occupied the island in 1906–1909.

21. The relationship between the U.S. and Cuba, thus, developed with strong political and economic ties. As with many Caribbean countries, including Haiti and the Dominican Republic, military dictatorships thrived in Cuba with the support of the U.S. Over the course of the relationship, there has been considerable travel between both countries, and the U.S. at times has exerted physical and political control over Cuba's affairs. After the Cuban Revolution of 1959 toppled the U.S. supported military dictatorship of Fulgencio Batista, approximately 690,000 Cubans were admitted to the U.S. as refugees under preferential rules that dispensed with the need for individual Cubans to establish refugee status under the 1951 United Nations (UN) Refugee Treaty. That Revolution, Cuba's increasingly amicable relationship to the then Soviet Union, and U.S. support of Cuban refugees' attempt to overthrow the dictatorship set up by revolutionary leader Fidel Castro, led to a complete and formal break-down in the relationship between both countries in 1961. The U.S. instituted an embargo on Cuba, including a ban on American travel to Cuba. Cuba, as a communist dictatorship, strictly controlled travel from Cuba. Throughout the latter half of the twentieth century, Cuban immigrants have made their way to the U.S. seeking refuge either from political persecution or dire economic need. In 1980, the Cuban government opened up its port in Mariel to Cubans wishing to leave the island. Hundreds of vessels sailed from Miami to Cuba to pick up Cubans, in defiance of U.S. law. Approximately 125,000 Cubans migrated to the U.S. during the Mariel boatlift. A slight 2% of that number had been imprisoned in Cuba for criminal activity or suffered from mental illness. Most Mariel Cubans were admitted as refugees and absorbed into the American community. The Carter administration and Cuba negotiated an agreement to regulate immigration to the U.S. from Cuba in 1984, but that agreement was suspended in 1985. Subsequently, the two countries have attempted to negotiate migration issues and resumption of diplomatic relations, with no permanent agreement being reached. The Obama administration initiated efforts to resume full diplomatic relations with Cuba. In May 2015, the U.S. removed Cuba from its list of State sponsors of terrorism. In 2017, then-President Obama terminated the policy that allowed Cubans who arrived on U.S. soil without visas to remain in the country and gain legal residency, known as the "wet foot, dry foot" policy. Thereafter, Cubans arriving without a visa in the U.S. were treated in the same way as all undocumented arrivals seeking refuge are treated: placed in removal proceedings but given an opportunity to apply for refugee status. Both countries pledged to normalize relations and the U.S. committed to work to reestablish an embassy in Havana. Subsequent efforts to normalize relations have stalled. The Trump administration reinstated the restrictions on travel and trade, which had been eased by the Obama administration. In addition, the Trump administration has reduced the number of embassy staff in Havana as a result of as yet unexplained injuries to American and Canadian diplomatic staff. The Biden administration has undertaken a review of U.S. policy on Cuba.

22. At the start of the twentieth century, the U.S. continued to experience strong immigration until the Great Depression, but the source countries changed somewhat, in part, due to passage of legislation that limited the number of persons allowed to migrate to the U.S. based on their country of origin. Thus, from 1901 to 1910, Italy (2 million) and the Soviet Union (1.5 million) were the source countries that dominated immigration to the U.S.; from 1911 to 1920, Italy (1.1 million), the Soviet Union (921,200), and Canada (742,200) were the top three source countries. From 1921 to 1930, Canada was the top source country (924,500), with Italy, Germany and Mexico trailing behind with approximately 400,000 individuals each. These numbers come from the government census. The census data prior to 1906 recorded the country the noncitizen came from, not necessarily whether the country was the noncitizen's place of birth. It was not until 1980 that census data on immigrants began to reflect the country of birth.

23. The strong wave of migration at the turn of the century prompted concerns about immigrants. In 1907 both houses of Congress established the U.S. Immigration Commission to study and make recommendations on immigration to the U.S. in 1911 the Dillingham Commission, as it came to be known, issued a forty-one-volume statistical report on immigration to the U.S., and concluded that immigration to the U.S. from southern and eastern Europe threatened American culture. The Dillingham Commission recommended the adoption of a literacy requirement for immigrants and sharp curtailment of immigration overall. The Dillingham Commission's report led to the racially restrictive immigration legislation of the 1920s. As a result of that legislation, immigration to the U.S. from the Eastern Hemisphere was limited to approximately 150,000. Migration from Asia was barred as well. Western Hemisphere countries, however, were not numerically restricted.

24. World War I generated nativist concerns about immigrants and a wave of hostility toward German immigrants. This war resulted in a good deal of propaganda directed at Germans and German culture. An "English only" movement emerged in the late 1910s and early 1920s. In 1903, only fourteen states required instruction to be in English; some allowed foreign language instruction. By 1923, thirty-five states required instruction in schools to be in English. After the end of World War I, twenty-two states prohibited the teaching of foreign languages in primary schools. A number of states prohibited the teaching of German and other foreign languages in secondary schools. In 1915, 24% of all high school students in the U.S. studied German; by 1922 less than 1% did.[3] This movement led to some of the first U.S. Supreme Court decisions recognizing that the liberty protected under the due process clause of the 14th Amendment included some specific fundamental rights not enumerated in the Bill of Rights like the right of parents to make certain decisions about their children's education. In *Meyer v. Nebraska*,[4] the Supreme Court invalidated a Nebraska statute that prohibited instruction in German except on the Sabbath in a house of worship. English only movements have continued to play a minimal role in the U.S.

25. The U.S. entered World War II as an Allied power, in response to Japan's attack on Pearl Harbor on December 7, 1941. This period transformed American

3. *See* Paul Finkelman, *German Victims and American Oppressors: The Cultural Background and Legacy of Meyer v. Nebraska*, in *Law and the Great Plains* (John Wunder ed., Greenwood Press 1996).
4. 262 U.S. 390 (1923).

society into a modern, industrialized world power; the period began with integration of the races through the military, and, eventually, the federal government, as well as the integration of women into the American workforce. Racial and ethnic fears, however, led to the forcible relocation and detention in concentration camps of USCs and Alien Admitted for Permanent Residence (LPRs) of Japanese origin for the duration of World War II. In 1942, President Roosevelt issued Executive Order 9066 authorizing the exclusion of anyone from any territory that military authorities determined was justified to protect national security without trial or hearings. Subsequently, the government forcibly relocated and interned approximately 110,000 persons born in Japan (Issei) or of Japanese ancestry (Nisei). Approximately two-thirds of those interned were USCs. The exclusion of American citizens of Japanese ethnicity or origin was upheld by the U.S. Supreme Court in *Korematsu v. United States.*[5] After World War II and the closing of the camps, the Japanese American community sought redress. In 1971, Congress enacted the Non-Detention Act, 18 U.S.C. (United States Code) §4001(a), which provides that "[n]o citizen shall be imprisoned or otherwise detained by the United States except pursuant to an Act of Congress." The act's legislative history made clear that Congress intended to prevent a repetition of the internments of Japanese Americans during World War II. In 1980, Congress established the Commission on Wartime Relocation and Internment of Civilians to study the issue. The Commission issued a report and formal recommendations in 1983 but it was not until 1988 that Congress passed the Civil Liberties Act of 1988, Pub. L. 100–383, 102 Stat. 903. This act acknowledged that the relocation and internment of civilians "were carried out without adequate security reasons and without any acts of espionage or sabotage documented ... , and were motivated largely by racial prejudice, wartime hysteria, and a failure of political leadership."[6] The act also conveyed a formal apology on behalf of the people of the U.S. to victims of internment; provided for a public education fund to finance efforts to inform the public about the internment and prevent its recurrence; and provided restitution to victims.[7] The government paid individual victims USD 20,000 with a signed apology from the President of the U.S.

26. Although the passage of the 13th, 14th, and 15th Amendments after the Civil War was intended to ensure that freed slaves were treated equally with other persons or citizens of the U.S., Southern states used forced segregation by law, and other practices, to deprive Black citizens of their vote and other fundamental and civil rights. It was not until the Supreme Court decided the case of *Brown v. Board of Education*[8] in 1954 that segregation in education was declared unconstitutional and a violation of the equal protection guarantee under the 14th Amendment and, subsequently, under the 5th Amendment. The *Brown* decision signaled the Civil Rights Era, a period dominated by strong political activity by groups disenchanted with American society and with American participation in the Vietnam War. The era

5. 323 U.S. 214 (1944).
6. 50 App. U.S.C. §1989a(a) (2003).
7. 50 App. U.S.C. §1989 (2003).
8. 347 U.S. 483 (1954).

generated recognition of strong constitutional protection for individual civil liberties, freedom from oppressive government and police action, and freedom from racial discrimination and discrimination on the basis of one's sex. Although the 19th Amendment, ensuring women suffrage, had been adopted in 1920, women still were deprived of basic fundamental civil and fundamental rights. In 1976, the U.S. Supreme Court recognized sex as a semi-suspect classification under the 14th Amendment equal protection clause and made it much more difficult for states and the federal government to discriminate on the basis of sex.

27. Throughout the twentieth century, documented migration to the U.S. continued to increase from a low of 528,000 in the 1930s to a high of 9 million in the 1990s. Between the 1930s and the 1950s, Germany was the leading source country. Since the 1960s, however, Mexico has been the leading source country of migrants to the U.S. Other high source countries include China, India and the Philippines.

28. Since the 1990s, the U.S. has admitted for permanent residence between 600,000 and approximately 1 million immigrants a year. Almost one-half of LPRs are immediate relatives of USCs. An additional fourth are admitted on the basis of an additional family relationship to a USC (older children or siblings of USCs) or on the basis of a family relationship (spouse or children) to a lawful permanent resident of the U.S. The remaining immigrants are admitted on the basis of an employment relationship, through a lottery, or as a refugee.

29. In 2010, for example, the U.S. admitted a total of 1,042,625 immigrants for permanent residence. Of those, 476,414 were immediate relatives (spouses and minor children of USCs); 214,589 were family-sponsored immigrants (unmarried sons/daughters of USCs, spouses and children of LPRs, married sons/daughters of USCs and siblings of USCs); 148,343 were employment sponsored; 49,763 were admitted through the diversity lottery; 92,741 were admitted as refugees; and 43,550 were admitted as asylees.

30. In 2011 the U.S. admitted a total of 1,062,040 immigrants for permanent residence. Of those, 453,158 were immediate relatives of USCs; 234,931 were family-sponsored immigrants; 139,339 were employment sponsored; 50,103 were admitted through the diversity lottery; 113,045 were admitted as refugees; and 55,415 were admitted as asylees.

31. In 2012 the U.S. admitted a total of 1,031,631 immigrants for permanent residence. Of those, 478,780 were immediate relatives of USCs; 202,019 were family-sponsored preferences; 143,998 were employment sponsored; 40,320 were diversity lottery admissions; 105,528 were refugee admissions; and 45,086 were admitted as asylees.

32. In 2013 the U.S. admitted 990,553 immigrants for permanent residence. Of those, 439,460 were immediate relatives of USCs; 210,303 were family-sponsored preferences; 161,110 were employment sponsored; 45,618 were diversity lottery admissions; 77,395 were admitted as refugees; and 42,235 were admitted as asylees.

33. In 2014, the U.S. admitted 1,016,518 immigrants for permanent residence. Of those, 416,456 were immediate relatives of USCs; 229,104 were family-sponsored preferences; 151,596 were employment preferences; 53,490 were diversity lottery admissions; 96,066 were refugees; and 38,176 were asylees.

34. In 2015, the U.S. admitted 1,051,031 immigrants for permanent residence. Of those, 465,068 were immediate relatives of USCs; 213,910 were family-sponsored preferences; 144,047 were employment preferences; 47,934 were diversity lottery admissions; 118,431 were refugees; and 33,564 were asylees.

35. In 2016, the U.S. admitted 1,183,505 immigrants for permanent residence. Of those, 566,706 were immediate relatives of USCs; 238,087 were family-sponsored preferences; 137,893 were employment preferences; 49,865 were diversity lottery admissions; 120,216 were refugees; and 37,209 were asylees.

36. In 2017, the U.S. admitted 1,127,167 immigrants for permanent residence. Of those, 516,508 were immediate relatives of USCs; 232,238 were family-sponsored preferences; 137,855 were employment preferences; 51,592 were diversity lottery admissions; 120,356 were refugees; and 25,647 were asylees.

37. In 2018, the U.S. admitted 1,096,611 immigrants for permanent residence. Of those, 478,961 were immediate relatives of USCs; 216,563 were family-sponsored preferences; 138,171 were employment preferences; 45,350 were diversity lottery admissions; 155,734 were refugees; and 30,175 were asylees.

38. Immigrants to the U.S. in recent decades are young and include both women and men. Most are from North America and Asia. Over 50% of the immigrants who were admitted into the U.S. in 2012 were women. One-third of immigrants were between the ages of 25 and 39. In 2013, the median age for permanent residents was 32 years, younger than the median age of the U.S. native population (35 years). The majority of new permanent residents were married (58%). Over two-thirds were from North America (315,660) and Asia (400,548). The trend appears to be descriptive of migration for the decade: over 50% (54%) of the immigrants who were admitted into the U.S. in 2016 were women. More than one-third (34.04%) of the immigrants were between the ages of 25 and 39 (2016). In 2016, the median age for permanent residents was 32 years, younger than the median age of the U.S. native population (36 years). The majority of new permanent residents were married (58.16%) (2016). Over two-thirds were from North America (427,293) and Asia (462,299) (2016).

39. The primary destination states for legal immigrants since 1971 are California, New York, Florida, Texas, New Jersey and Illinois. The top metropolitan destinations for immigrants in 2013 were New York-Northern New Jersey-Long Island, NY-NJ-PA; Los Angeles-Long Beach-Santa Ana, California; Miami-Fort

Lauderdale-Pompano Beach, Florida; Washington-Arlington-Alexandria, D.C.-Virginia-Maryland-West Virginia; Chicago-Joliet-Naperville, Illinois-Indiana-Wisconsin; Houston-Sugar Land-Baytown, and San Francisco-Oakland-Fremont, California. Forty-five percent of new permanent residents in 2013 resided in these metropolitan areas.

40. In addition to approximately 1 million documented immigrants, some number of irregular immigrants settle in the U.S. annually either through unauthorized entry or through entry as temporary visitors who stay after their visa has expired. In 2014, the government estimated that approximately 12.1 million unauthorized or undocumented immigrants resided in the U.S. More recent estimates by the Pew Research Center, however, suggest that border crossings have been reduced substantially and that the number of unauthorized or undocumented immigrants in the U.S. dropped to approximately 10.7 million in 2016. That represented approximately 3.3% of the total U.S. population in 2016. Fifty-eight percent of unauthorized immigrants reside in six states: California, Texas, Florida, New York, New Jersey and Illinois. Approximately two-thirds of unauthorized or undocumented immigrants have resided in the U.S. for more than ten years. Currently, the majority of unauthorized or undocumented immigrants are persons who have overstayed their visa, rather than entrants crossing the U.S./Mexico border.

41. The U.S. government deports a substantial number of unauthorized or undocumented immigrants every year. In addition, the U.S. also deports permanent resident immigrants who have subsequently become removable. For example, in 2011, the government detained 429,247 foreign nationals pending deportation through a process called removal; the government actually removed 387,134 foreign nationals. In 2012, the number of detained and removed foreign nationals increased substantially to 477,523 (detained) and 418,397 (removed). In 2013 approximately 440,557 noncitizens were detained and almost the same number, 438,421, were removed, an all-time high. The majority of foreign nationals removed are from Mexico. For example, 72% of persons removed in 2013 were from Mexico. Almost one-half of removals (44%) in 2013 were accomplished through a process called expedited removal. Expedited removal offers much less procedural protection to noncitizens than the formal removal process.

42. The U.S. Department of Homeland Security (DHS) reports noncitizens who are deported as either removed (pursuant to a formal order of removal) or returned (not based on an order of removal). Persons who are removed pursuant to a formal order of removal are subject to possible criminal charges if they reenter the U.S. without authorization.

43. In 2013 the U.S. Bureau of Immigration and Customs Enforcement (ICE) removed approximately 433,034 noncitizens, and an additional 178,663 noncitizens were returned. A total of 277,277 new cases were filed by DHS in immigration courts. Immigration courts completed 254,197 cases. In majority of those cases (99,664 cases or 69.3%), the immigration court ordered the noncitizen removed. In 16.7% (24,031) of the cases, the immigration court granted relief from removal and the rest were either terminated or resulted in other dispositions. As in other years, the majority of noncitizens placed in removal proceedings were not represented by counsel. In 2013 counsel (or an accredited representative or some other individual permitted to appear in immigration court) represented approximately 59% of noncitizens in completed immigration court proceedings. Generally, there is a higher rate of legal representation for noncitizens in administrative appellate proceedings. In 2013 counsel represented approximately 79% of completed cases before the Board of Immigration Appeals (BIA). Very few cases, however, are appealed to the BIA. In 2013, approximately 11% of immigration judge's decisions were appealed to the BIA. In 2014 approximately 10% of immigration court decisions were administratively appealed.

44. During the last two years of the Obama administration, the pace of removals slowed to 326,962 pursuant to an order of removal and 129,429 returned in 2015, and in 2016, 340,046 removals pursuant to an order of removal and 106,167 returned. The 2017 statistics released by ICE report 226,119 removals, a decrease from the prior year. Arrests and detentions, however, appear to have increased. ICE attributed the decrease in removal numbers in 2017 to the decline in border apprehensions. ICE reported 295,052 new removal cases filed by DHS in immigration court, and thus the number of cases filed for removal has increased. Immigration courts in 2017 completed 169,150 cases.

45. During the Trump administration, the number of removals and returns initially declined. ICE removed 288,093 noncitizens in 2017 and returned 100,708 noncitizens. In 2018, however, removals and returns were similar to the last two years of the previous administration. ICE removed 337,287 noncitizens and returned 108,083 noncitizens in 2018.

46. Temporary admissions to the U.S. are considered as nonimmigrant admissions. Nonimmigrant admissions include tourists and temporary business visitors; temporary workers and students; and temporary visa holders who are expected to become long-term residents, like fiancés of U.S. citizens and their children. Generally, the U.S. admits many more nonimmigrants than immigrants. While immigrant admissions hover around 1 million annually, total nonimmigrant admissions for the past three years have hovered around 180 million annually. In 2015, for example, the U.S. admitted a total of 181,300,000 nonimmigrants; in 2016, the U.S. admitted 178,700,000; in 2017, the U.S. admitted 181,100,000 nonimmigrants; and in 2018, the U.S. admitted 186,200,000 nonimmigrants. The largest category of temporary admissions are tourists. For example, according to U.S. government statistics, in 2015, the U.S. admitted a total of 61,017,237 temporary visitors for pleasure (tourists). In 2016, the U.S. admitted 61,029,117 tourists. In 2017, the total temporary visitors for pleasure admissions was 61,600,219. In 2018, it admitted 64,819,854 tourists. These numbers do not include short-term admissions from Canada and Mexico. The largest categories of temporary admissions are work-related, including approximately 8 million annual temporary visitors for business, and almost 4 million annual admissions for temporary workers and their families. The U.S. admits almost 2 million students annually.

47. Approximately three-fourth million immigrants become USCs every year. In 2013, 779,929 persons naturalized; subsequently, the numbers have decreased slightly. In 2014, 653,416 persons naturalized, and in 2015, 730,259 persons naturalized. In 2016, the number of persons to naturalize rose again to 753,060, but the number decreased again in 2017, dropping down to 707,265. In 2018, 761,901 permanent residents naturalized. Petitions for naturalization have been increasing for the past few years: in 2016, 972,151 persons filed a petition to naturalize and in 2017, 986,851 persons filed for naturalization. In 2018, however, the number of petitions filed dropped with only 810,548 petitions. During that same period, approximately 80,000 petitions for naturalization were denied annually. In 2018, however, the number of petitions denied rose significantly: the government denied 92,586 petitions.

48. According to the 2010 Census Bureau figures, approximately 12.9% (39,956,000) of the U.S. population (308,745,538) are foreign-born. Approximately 5.6% (17,476,000) of the foreign-born are USCs and 7.3% (22,480,000) are noncitizens. The Census Bureau's survey included lawful permanent residents, temporary migrants, humanitarian migrants, and unauthorized migrants within the category of noncitizens. Treating both Census (approximately 22 million noncitizens) and DHS estimates (11 million unauthorized/undocumented migrants) as accurate suggests that 50% of the noncitizens in the U.S. are here without authorization. Whether accurate or not, these numbers influenced the perception that unauthorized migration is a problem for the U.S. This perception has generated substantial state and local government regulation of immigration-related offenses, and in some cases, status offenses, generally disfavored under traditional American legal principles. In addition to enacting new legislation, state and local law enforcement officials have stepped up enforcement efforts directed at unauthorized noncitizens. These efforts have generated substantial litigation; the extent to which states and local communities are authorized to regulate immigrants is unsettled and may depend on federal statutes and the U.S. Constitution. State regulation of immigration and noncitizens through criminal and civil law varies from state to state and is therefore beyond the scope of this monograph.

49. According to the U.S. Census Bureau, Hispanic and Latinx are the second-largest ethnic group in the U.S., after non-Hispanic White Americans. As of the 2010 U.S. Census, the population of the U.S. totaled 308,745,538 million: non-Hispanic White Americans were the majority at 196.8 million; followed by Hispanics or Latinx at 50.5 million; followed by Blacks or African Americans at 37.7 million; Asians at 14.5 million; American Indians and Alaska natives at 2.2 million; and native Hawaiians and other Pacific Islanders at half a million. Four states (Hawaii, New Mexico, California and Texas) and the District of Columbia were "majority-minority" states (more than 50% of their population is made up of people other than single-race non-Hispanic Whites).

§2. Overview of National Legal Instruments

I. Historical Overview

50. The legislative branch of government—Congress—established by the U.S. Constitution, first acted to authorize the executive branch of government—the President—to use the power to deport noncitizens in 1798, shortly after the adoption of the Constitution. The Aliens Act of June 25, 1798,[9] authorized the President to arrest and/or deport any alien whom he deemed dangerous to the U.S. and required the captain of any vessel to report the arrival of aliens on board such vessel to the chief officer of the customs of the port. This law expired two years after its enactment. The Alien Enemy Act of July 6, 1798,[10] granted the President, in the case of a declared war or invasion, the power to restrain or remove alien enemy males of 14 years and upward, with due protection of their property rights as stipulated by the treaty. This act is still in effect today. In 1808, Congress enacted a statute banning the importation of slaves into the U.S. Eleven years later, Congress passed the Steerage Act of March 2, 1819,[11] a statute requiring vessels arriving in the U.S. to keep and provide passenger records, thus, facilitating the recordation of arrivals in the U.S. In the years leading up to the Civil War, Congress passed a series of statutes protecting passengers and, in 1855, distinguishing between permanent and temporary immigrants in reports to the Secretary of State. During the Civil War, in 1864, Congress provided for a Commissioner of Immigration to be appointed by the President, to serve under the Secretary of State, and authorized immigrant labor contracts that allowed would-be immigrants to pledge one year's labor in return for transportation to the U.S.[12] This act was repealed in 1868. It was not until after the Civil War and the prohibition against slavery adopted by the 13th Amendment to the U.S. that Congress enacted statutes restricting entry into the country.

51. The first federal regulation of entry into the U.S. was enacted in 1875 and excluded prostitutes and convicts from admission.[13] The Act of 1882,[14] further excluded lunatics, idiots, and those liable to become a public charge. Also in 1882, Congress enacted the Chinese Exclusion Act,[15] which suspended immigration of Chinese laborers to the U.S. for ten years, prohibited admitting Chinese for citizenship and provided for the deportation of Chinese found unlawfully within the U.S. The act provided for the issuance of certificates of identity to those Chinese laborers already in the U.S. preserving their right to reenter the U.S. after a temporary absence. Congress prohibited contract labor into the U.S. in the Act of February 26,

9. 1 Statutes-at-Large 570.
10. 1 Statutes-at-Large 577.
11. 3 Statutes-at-Large 488.
12. Act of Jul. 4, 1864, 13 Statutes-at-Large 385.
13. Act of Mar. 3, 1875, 18 Statutes-at-Large 477.
14. 22 Statutes-at-Large 214.
15. 22 Statutes-at-Large 58.

1885,[16] and in 1887 amended the statute to provide for enforcement by the Secretary of the Treasury. In the Act of 1888,[17] Congress, however, prohibited the return of all Chinese laborers who had left the U.S. temporarily even if they had been issued certificates of identity. This statute was challenged on constitutional grounds by a returning long-term Chinese resident of the U.S. who had departed the U.S. and sought reentry with a certificate of identity. The statute was upheld by the U.S. Supreme Court in *Chae Chan Ping v. United States*,[18] as a valid exercise of Congressional powers to control entry into the U.S. In the Immigration Act of March 3, 1891,[19] Congress added to the classes of persons inadmissible to the U.S. and excluded persons with contagious diseases as well as polygamists; the act also expanded the kinds of criminal offenses that would render persons inadmissible. In addition, the statute established the Bureau of Immigration under the Treasury Department to administer immigration laws and provided for the deportation of any alien who entered the U.S. unlawfully. The Chinese Exclusion Act did not apply to diplomatic and other officers of the Chinese Government, including their household persons. In addition, exceptions were made for merchants, students, teachers, and travelers.

52. At the beginning of the twentieth century, Congress transferred the Bureau of Immigration from the Treasury Department to the Department of Commerce and Labor.[20] Immigration regulation reflected concerns and responses to the Russian Revolution and the outbreak of World War I. In the Immigration Act of March 3, 1903,[21] Congress added to the classes of inadmissible aliens, in particular, anarchists, and persons who believe in, or advocate, the overthrow by force or violence of the government of the U.S. In the Naturalization Act of June 29, 1906,[22] Congress combined the immigration and naturalization functions of the federal government in the Bureau of Immigration and Naturalization, still within the Department of Commerce. Congress undertook codification of earlier immigration legislation in 1907.[23] This act again expanded the classes of inadmissible persons and created a Joint Commission on Immigration. In 1910, the White Slave Traffic Act, also known as the Mann Act,[24] prohibited the importation or interstate transportation of women for immoral purposes. In the Act of March 4, 1913,[25] Congress separated the commerce and labor departments and transferred the immigration and naturalization functions to a new Department of Labor (DOL). Congress also separated the immigration and naturalization functions and established a Bureau of Immigration and a Bureau of Naturalization, each headed by its own Commissioner. Subsequently, in 1917, Congress further restricted the immigration of Asian persons (the Chinese

16. 23 Statutes-at-Large 332.
17. 25 Statutes-at-Large 566.
18. 130 U.S. 581 (1889).
19. 26 Statutes-at-Large 1084.
20. Act of Feb. 14, 1903, 32 Statutes-at-Large 825.
21. 32 Statutes-at-Large 1213.
22. 34 Statutes-at-Large 596.
23. Immigration Act of Feb. 20, 1907, 343 Statutes-at-Large 898.
24. 36 Statutes-at-Large 825.
25. 37 Statutes-at-Large 737.

Exclusion Acts were in effect until 1943). Congress continued to expand the classes of excludable persons, including those who were illiterate. Congress also provided for deportation of certain classes of persons without a statute of limitation.[26] The Act of May 22, 1918,[27] authorized the President to control departure and entry in times of war or national emergency of any noncitizen whose presence was contrary to public safety.

53. In the Quota Law of May 19, 1921,[28] Congress provided for the first quantitative restriction on immigrants. The statute limited the number of aliens of any nationality entering the U.S. to 3% of the foreign-born persons of that nationality who lived in the U.S. in 1910; thus, this act introduced the national origins system of immigration, made permanent in the Immigration Act of May 26, 1924.[29] That act established a national origins quota system for immigrants from the Eastern Hemisphere (primarily Europeans, since Asians were barred from admission for the most part) and gave preferred quota status to unmarried children under 21 of U.S. citizens, parents of U.S. citizens, and spouses of U.S. citizens aged 21 and over. The act exempted wives (not husbands), unmarried children under 18 of U.S. citizens and natives of Western Hemisphere countries, among others, from the quotas. The 1924 Act, thus, formally introduced the concept of family-based immigration, upon which current immigration law is based. The act also established the system, still essentially in effect, of consular control by prohibiting noncitizens from entering the U.S. without a visa issued by an American consular officer abroad. Thus, the act placed authority for immigration with the Department of State (DOS), in the issuance of visas, and with the DOL. Also in 1924, Congress provided for the establishment of the U.S. Border Patrol.[30]

54. In the Act of June 14, 1940,[31] Congress transferred the Immigration and Naturalization Service from the DOL to the Department of Justice (DOJ), where it remained until 2003, when administration of immigration and naturalization laws was placed under the DHS. Also in 1940, Congress enacted the Alien Registration Act of June 28, 1940,[32] which required registration of all noncitizens and fingerprinting of all those over 14 years of age. The statute also expanded the classes of excludable and deportable aliens to include those who had been members, in the past, of prohibited organizations, like the Communist Party.

55. World War II generated a number of immigration legislation measures, including legislative provisions to facilitate the entry of temporary agricultural

---

26. Immigration Act of Feb. 5, 1917, 39 Statutes-at-Large 874.
27. 40 Statutes-at-Large 559.
28. 42 Statutes-at-Large 5.
29. 43 Statutes-at-Large 153.
30. Act of May 28, 1924, 43 Statutes-at-Large 240.
31. 54 Statutes-at-Large 230.
32. 54 Statutes-at-Large 670.

workers from Mexico and other North, Central and South American countries, eventually known as the Mexican "Bracero Program."[33] The goal of the program was to import short-term agricultural workers to replace the labor shortage caused by the war. The program began as a series of bilateral agreements with Mexico in 1942. It was terminated in 1964. It is estimated that foreign workers signed 4.6 million contracts, many returning to the U.S. several times on different contracts, making it the largest U.S. temporary foreign worker program.[34] The Bracero Program proved to be a controversial program; it resulted in worker abuse and facilitated exploitation of Mexican workers. In addition, the U.S. government forcibly deported many workers admitted to the U.S. under the Bracero Program. Some USCs were forcibly deported as well.

56. During World War II era, Congress also amended the Alien Registration Act of 1940 to repeal the Chinese Exclusion laws and provide for the naturalization of Chinese persons or persons of Chinese descent, Act of December 17, 1943,[35] and persons from India and the Philippines, Act of July 2, 1946.[36] After 1940, immigration from Asian countries increased. Between 1940 and 1949, 34,532 immigrants from Asia were admitted for permanent residency, an increase of 79% from the previous decade numbers.

57. Congress also facilitated immigration of spouses of members of the armed forces of the U.S. through the War Brides Act of December 28, 1945.[37]

58. World War II resulted in more than one million displaced persons in refugee camps throughout Europe, with most left homeless and stateless. Congress enacted the first statute to specifically provide for admission of refugees, the Displaced Persons Act of June 25, 1948,[38] which permitted admission of 205,000 displaced persons to be charged against future immigrant quotas. Subsequent statutes increased the number of refugees who could be admitted. Until the enactment of the Refugee Act of March 17, 1980,[39] the U.S. dealt with refugee admissions through targeted, narrow legislation such as the Fair Share Refugee Act, Act of July 14, 1960;[40] the

33. Act of Apr. 29, 1943, 57 Statutes-at-Large 70; Agricultural Act of Oct. 31, 1949, 63 Statutes-at-Large 1051 (extending Bracero Program); Act of Jul. 12, 1951, 65 Statutes-at-Large 119 (providing limited protection to Bracero workers); Act of Feb. 14, 1944, 58 Statutes-at-Large 11 (providing for temporary workers in other industries).
34. Gilberto Cardenas, United States Immigration Policy Toward Mexico: An Historical Perspective, 2 Chicano L. Rev. 66, 75 (1975).
35. 57 Statutes-at-Large 600.
36. 60 Statutes-at-Large 416.
37. 59 Statutes-at-Large 659.
38. 62 Statutes-at-Large 1009.
39. 94 Statutes-at-Large 102.
40. 74 Statutes-at-Large 504.

Act of November 2, 1966[41] (Cubans); the Indochina Migration and Refugee Assistance Act of May 23, 1975[42] (Cambodians and Vietnamese); the Act of June 21, 1976[43] (Laotians).

59. The Cold War generated more restrictive immigration provisions directed at Communist Party membership. The Internal Security Act of September 22, 1950[44] added former or current membership in the Communist party or any other totalitarian party as a ground for inadmissibility. Additionally, membership in the Communist party also rendered a noncitizen deportable, regardless of the length of time she/he had resided in the U.S.. The U.S. Supreme Court's view of fundamental or basic human rights during this period tended to be narrow. Many challenges to restrictive legislative and executive acts failed. For example, the Supreme Court upheld the indefinite detention of a stateless, returning permanent resident without a hearing in the case of *Shaughnessey v. Mezei*.[45] The Supreme Court distinguished between Mr. Mezei, absent from the U.S. for nineteen months, and permanent residents with shorter periods of absence like the noncitizen in *Kwong Hai Chew v. Colding*,[46] absent for only four months; the Supreme Court held that the latter were entitled to a hearing. In *Knauff v. Shaughnessy*,[47] the Supreme Court upheld the government's refusal to admit the spouse of a U.S. citizen without a hearing on the basis of secret evidence. Both of these individuals were eventually allowed to reside in the U.S. The Court also upheld the detention and deportation of many former Communist Party members despite their close relation to USCs and the fact that they appeared to be model residents of the U.S. at the time the government moved to deport them (*Galvan v. Press*,[48] *Carlson v. Landon*,[49] *Harisiades v. Shaughnessy*).[50]

60. In 1952, Congress acted to criminalize bringing in or willfully inducing a noncitizen to enter or reside in the U.S. who was not authorized to do so.[51]

61. More importantly, in 1952, Congress enacted comprehensive immigration legislation in the Immigration and Nationality Act of June 27, 1952 (the INA).[52] Although the 1952 INA continued the basic national origins quota system, it revised it substantially and eliminated race as a bar to immigration. This statute provided for family-based immigration and employment-based immigration. It established a numerical limitation of 150,000 immigrants from the Eastern Hemisphere; immigration from the Western Hemisphere remained uncapped. It also expanded the

41. 80 Statutes-at-Large 1161.
42. 89 Statutes-at-Large 87.
43. 90 Statutes-at-Large 691.
44. 64 Statutes-at-Large 987.
45. 345 U.S. 206 (1953).
46. 344 U.S. 590 (1953).
47. 338 U.S. 537 (1950).
48. 347 U.S. 522 (1954).
49. 342 U.S. 524 (1952).
50. 342 U.S. 580 (1952).
51. Act of Mar. 20, 1952, 66 Statutes-at-Large 26.
52. 66 Statutes-at-Large 163.

grounds for exclusion and deportation of noncitizens and provided additional procedural safeguards to aliens subject to deportation.

62. The U.S. formally abolished the national origins quota system with the INA Amendments of October 3, 1965,[53] thus, eliminating national origin, race or ancestry as a basis for immigration to the U.S. The act was one of several federal statutes to formally prohibit invidious discrimination against disfavored classifications like race or national origin. The Civil Rights Act of 1964[54] generally prohibited discrimination on the basis of race and national origin in housing, education and employment. Title VII of the Civil Rights Act prohibited discrimination in employment on the basis of race, national origin, color, sex and religion.[55] The 1965 INA maintained a numerical cap on migration from the Eastern Hemisphere (170,000) and applied a numerical cap for the first time to the Western Hemisphere (120,000). In addition, the INA established per-country limits on Eastern Hemisphere countries. The act established a seven-category preference system for immigrant visa based on family reunification or employment needs. The act established two categories of immigrants not subject to the numerical caps: immediate relatives of U.S. citizens (spouses, children and parents) and certain special immigrants. For employment-based visa, the act introduced a requirement that the Secretary of Labor declares that admission of the worker would not adversely affect the wages and working conditions of similarly employed individuals in the U.S. and that the worker would not displace a worker in the U.S. In 1976, Congress acted to apply the per-country limit on visas to countries in the Western Hemisphere, as well as the seven-category preference system.[56] This measure had a dramatic effect on immigration from Mexico and other countries geographically close to the U.S. and in which the U.S. historically had intervened. They became subject to the same per-country caps as countries geographically distant to the U.S. and with few or no ties to the U.S. In 1978, Congress eliminated separate ceilings for Eastern and Western Hemisphere immigration and provided for a worldwide limit of 290,000 immigrant visas.

63. In 1980, Congress passed legislation to provide a separate and systematic procedure for the admission and resettlement of refugees in conformance with the UN Convention Relating to the Status of Refugees and the 1967 Protocol on Refugees. The Refugee Act of March 17, 1980,[57] eliminated refugees as a category of the preference system and exempted refugees from the worldwide ceiling on immigration to the U.S. The Refugee Act defined the term "refugee" in conformance with the 1967 Protocol and provided for adjustment to permanent resident status of refugees who have been physically present in the U.S. for at least one year, and of asylees one year after asylum is granted.

---

53. 79 Statutes-at-Large 911.
54. Pub. L. 88-352, 78 Statutes-at-Large 253.
55. 42 U.S.C. §§2000e-2000e-17 (2003).
56. Immigration and Nationality Act Amendments of Oct. 20, 1976, 90 Statutes-at-Large 2703.
57. 94 Statutes-at-Large 102.

II. Current Applicable Legislation

64. The major federal statutes that regulate immigration today include the Refugee Act of March 17, 1980,[58] the Immigration Reform and Control Act of November 6, 1986 (IRCA),[59] the Immigration Marriage Fraud Amendments of November 10, 1986 (IMFA),[60] the Immigration Act of November 29, 1990 (INA),[61] the Anti-terrorism and Effective Death Penalty Act of April 24, 1996 (AEDPA),[62] the Personal Responsibility and Work Opportunity Reconciliation Act of August 22, 1996 (PRWORA),[63] the Illegal Immigration Reform and Immigrant Responsibility Act of September 30, 1996 (IIRIRA),[64] the Uniting and Strengthening America by Providing Appropriate Tools Required to Intercept and Obstruct Terrorism Act of 2001 (USA Patriot Act),[65] the Homeland Security Act of 2002,[66] and the Real ID Act of 2005.[67] Other statutes that have had an impact on immigration policy include the Secure Fence Act of 2006.[68]

65. The IRCA prohibited employment of unauthorized workers in the U.S. and imposed record-keeping duties on employers to verify that all workers employed have authorization to work. Employers who knowingly hire, recruit or refer for a fee noncitizens not authorized to work in the U.S. may be fined or, in certain cases, subject to imprisonment. IRCA also provided a legalization program for noncitizens who had resided in the U.S. without authorization (entering without inspection or as visa overstays) since January 1, 1982, and who were not inadmissible (excludable). IRCA also created a nonimmigrant visa waiver pilot program, expanded in the 1990 amendments to the INA, that allow certain noncitizens to visit the U.S. without applying for a nonimmigrant visa.

66. The IMFA prohibited both USCs and noncitizens from entering into a marriage for the purpose of gaining a benefit under U.S. immigration law. IMFA made such a marriage a criminal violation, and declared, for purposes of immigration law, such a marriage to be invalid and fraudulent. To discourage marriage for the purpose of conveying an immigration benefit, the statute made those who seek an immigrant visa on the basis of a marriage of less than two years as conditional immigrants. To remove conditional status, the couple must jointly petition for removal of the conditional status at the end of two years after receiving conditional status. The IMFA provided discretionary exceptions to the joint petition requirement in cases involving extreme hardship or where the marriage had been entered

58. Pub. L. 96-212, 94 Statutes-at-Large 102.
59. Pub. L. 99-603, 100 Statutes-at-Large 3359.
60. Pub. L. 99-639, 100 Statutes-at-Large 3537.
61. Pub. L. 101-649, 104 Statutes-at-Large 4978.
62. Pub. L. 104-132, 110 Statutes-at-Large 1214.
63. Pub. L. 104-193, 110 Statutes-at-Large 2105.
64. Pub. L. 104-208, 110 Statutes-at-Large 3009.
65. Pub. L. 107-56, 115 Statutes-at-Large 272 (USA PATRIOT Act).
66. Pub. L. 107-296, 116 Statutes-at-Large 2135 (2002).
67. Pub. L. 109-13, 119 Statutes-at-Large 231 (2005).
68. Pub. L. 109-367, 120 Stat. 2638 (2006).

into in good faith but subsequently had broken down and the spouse had good cause to divorce, thus, preventing the joint filing.

67. The 1990 amendments to the INA made substantial changes to immigration law and increased the overall number of visas annually available to immigrants from 290,000 to approximately 675,000. The majority of those visas (480,000) are reserved for family-sponsored immigrants; 140,000 are reserved for immigrants on the basis of employment; and 55,000 are reserved for "diversity immigrants," immigrants whose country of origin is not a source of a large number of immigrants to the U.S. The 1990 amendments also revised and reorganized the grounds of exclusion and deportation; established new nonimmigrant admission categories; authorized the Attorney General to grant temporary protected status (TPS) to undocumented noncitizens of designated countries under certain circumstances like armed conflict or natural disasters and transferred jurisdiction to naturalize immigrants from federal and state courts, to the Attorney General. The 1990 Act also provided relief to noncitizen spouses in abusive relationships adversely impacted by the conditional status provisions imposed by the IMFA. The Act provided a specific waiver from the joint petition to remove conditional status requirement for spouses who were subject to battering or extreme cruelty by their USC or LPR spouse.

68. The Violence Against Women Act of 1994 (VAWA), enacted as part of the Violent Crime Control and Law Enforcement Act of 1994,[69] and designed to respond comprehensively to domestic or intimate violence throughout the U.S., provided special protection for battered immigrant women and children. VAWA provisions recognized that the IMFA's requirement that a joint petition be filed imposed a substantial burden on battered spouses and gave the USC or LPR sponsoring spouse undue control over the spouse's immigrant status. Thus, VAWA specifically authorized the immigrant spouse and children in abusive relationships to self-petition for lawful immigrant status without the approval, assistance or cooperation of their abusive spouse or parent. The VAWA self-petition provisions are gender-neutral and, thus, available to spouses of either sex as long as they qualify. In order to qualify for relief, a spouse must be married to a USC or LPR at the time they file for lawful immigrant status; must prove that she/he has suffered battering or extreme cruelty; that the marriage was entered in good faith; that she/he resided with the USC or LPR spouse for a certain period of time; that she/he is of good moral character and that she/he and/or the children would suffer extreme hardship if deported.

69. In 1996 Congress passed three statutes, the AEDPA, the PRWORA and the IIRIRA, to target entry and deportation of noncitizens with ties to terrorism; to minimize judicial review of administrative immigration decisions; to reduce the benefits available to noncitizens, in particular, noncitizens admitted as permanent residents to the U.S.; to create a new removal process to replace the existing exclusion and deportation processes; to facilitate expedited process for removal of certain categories of noncitizens; and, among other things, to provide for mandatory detention of certain categories of deportable noncitizens. Two of these statutes, AEDPA and the

69. Pub. L. 103-322, 108 Statutes-at-Large 1796.

PRWORA, were not primarily immigration statutes. Nonetheless, the statutes modified immigration process substantially and further restricted the categories of persons eligible to enter the U.S., or to qualify for permanent residence in the U.S. and to remain in the U.S., after being admitted for permanent residence. The AEDPA expanded the categories of excludable noncitizens related to terrorist activity, facilitated and expedited the deportation of noncitizens rendered deportable because of criminal activity, including non-violent criminal activity, limited judicial review of deportation orders, and authorized state and local enforcement of federal immigration laws through cooperative agreements between the U.S. government and local/ state governments.

70. The PRWORA enacted a reworking of the federal welfare benefits system. Its immigration-related provisions barred most noncitizens, including permanent resident immigrants, from participation in federally financed public welfare financial assistance, like food stamps and supplemental security income, and made it possible for states to deny immigrants participation in either federal or state-funded programs. Permanent residents are eligible for federal student financial aid. Permanent residents are also eligible for social security benefits. In addition, the PRWORA denied unauthorized noncitizens and nonimmigrants (temporary residents) access to most federal, state and local public benefits.

71. The IIRIRA targeted immigration reform to reduce unauthorized migration to the U.S. and strengthened immigration enforcement efforts. The statute continued the trend to engage state and local law enforcement in cooperative or complementary efforts to enforce immigration laws. For example, it initiated a pilot program that allowed states to deny driver's licenses to unauthorized noncitizens. The statute also created a new process through which to deport or exclude noncitizens in the interior of the U.S. or attempting entry. This process, which is called "removal," replaced exclusion and deportation hearings and provided for the same statutory procedural protection for noncitizens charged with being inadmissible to or deportable from the U.S. The statute also provided for "expedited" removal of a number of classes of aliens, primarily arriving noncitizens, with reduced procedural protections. The statute also provided three-and ten-year bars to admissibility for noncitizens seeking to reenter the U.S. after having been removed from the U.S. or after having resided in the U.S. without authorization. The statute also expanded the grounds of inadmissibility and deportability and substantially revised procedures and criteria for granting asylum to refugees. Moreover, the statute provided new restrictions on judicial review of removal and discretionary immigration administrative decisions. To an extent, in enacting these statutes, Congress was reacting to incidents of terrorist activity directed at the U.S., including the first attempt to destroy the World Trade Center in 1993, and the bombing of the Oklahoma City Federal Building in 1995.

72. The VAWA 2000, enacted as part of the Victims of Trafficking and Violence Protection Act of 2000,[70] for the first time provided protection and some relief to noncitizen victims of sexual assault, trafficking and other crimes. In addition, VAWA 2000 provided further relief to immigrant spouses and children of USCs or LPRs in abusive relationships. The VAWA 2000 lessened the evidentiary requirements of immigrants pursuing relief under VAWA; expanded the categories of immigrant spouses afforded VAWA relief; and expanded protection of abused children or children of abused spouses. In addition, VAWA 2000 makes it possible for VAWA immigrant self-petitioners to become lawful permanent residents while remaining safely in the U.S. The Violence Against Women and Department of Justice Reauthorization Act of 2005 (VAWA 2005),[71] included the International Marriage Broker Regulation Act of 2005 (IMBRA), which sought to protect noncitizen women at risk for domestic violence from USCs or LPRs seeking "mail order brides." IMBRA provisions require covered international marriage brokers to conduct background checks on U.S. clients and to provide information to participating noncitizens. Not all international matchmaking organizations are covered, however. The Violence Against Women Reauthorization Act of 2013[72] strengthened protection for individuals in the U.S. from gender-based violence, including domestic violence, sexual assault and stalking, with special provisions for Native American women, lesbian, gay, bisexual and transgender individuals, college students and immigrants.

73. The Trafficking Victims Protection Act of 2000, also part of the Victims of Trafficking and Violence Protection Act of 2000,[73] sought to provide a comprehensive response to the problem of human trafficking, including sex trafficking and international human trafficking. The statute created special nonimmigrant visa categories for victims of crime, in particular, victims of trafficking, who are assisting in the investigation or prosecution of these crimes. The Trafficking Victims Protection Act created the T visa for victims of severe trafficking in persons, including sex trafficking, who are physically present in the U.S. as a result of such trafficking; who assist in the investigation or prosecution of those trafficking acts; and who would suffer extreme hardship involving unusual and severe harm if removed from the U.S. That act also created the U visa for victims of criminal activity who have suffered substantial physical or mental abuse and who have assisted or may assist in the investigation or prosecution of the crime. The T visa and U visa provide for nonimmigrant status for three years. Visa holders may apply for an adjustment of their status after three years in that status. The maximum number of T visas available annually is 5,000. The maximum number of "U visas" available annually is 10,000 for primary applicants. There is no cap for spouses, children and parents of children under the age of 16 of U visa recipients, if they establish that receipt of a visa is necessary to avoid extreme hardship; or a government official certifies that investigation or prosecution would suffer without the assistance of the spouse, child, or

70. Pub. L. 106-386, 114 Statutes-at-Large 1464.
71. Pub. L. 109-162, 119 Stat. 2960 (2006).
72. Pub. L. 113-4, 127 Stat. 54 (2013).
73. Pub. L. 106-386, 114 Statutes-at-Large 1464.

parent of a nonimmigrant child. The government did not issue regulations implementing the U nonimmigrant visa until 2007. The VAWA of 2005[74] extended the duration of U visa status from three years to four years. Thus, noncitizens granted U visa status may reside in the U.S. for a maximum of four years in that status and may adjust to permanent residency after three years of continuous presence in the U.S. in U status, as long as they are in valid U nonimmigrant status. Recent amendments in the William Wilberforce Trafficking Victims Protection Reauthorization Act of 2008 (TVPRA)[75] provide for an extension of time under certain circumstances: if the Secretary of DHS determines an extension is warranted due to exceptional circumstances, the noncitizen is eligible for adjustment under §245(m) of the INA but cannot adjust because implementing regulations have not been issued, and while an application for adjustment under §245(m) is pending. Since 2008, United States Bureau of Citizenship and Immigration Services (USCIS) has approved the statutory maximum of 10,000 U visas. In 2015, USCIS approved the maximum number of U visas available for 2015 by the end of January 2015. In 2017, 36,531 U visa petitions were received and 10,031 were approved. A total of 2,128 U visa applications were denied. Once USCIS approves the maximum number of U visas available for that fiscal year, eligible U visa applicants are placed on a waiting list and granted deferred action or parole and work authorization while they wait for a U visa to become available. U visa applicants on the waiting list must be eligible for the U Visa at the time it is issued. In 2017, 110,511 petitions for U visas were pending. In 2018, 58,991 U visa petitions were filed: of that number 17,915 were approved and 4,308 denied. As of 2020, there are over 200,000 U visa petitions pending.

74. The terrorist attacks of September 11, 2001 on the World Trade Center in New York City and the Pentagon in Washington D.C. stimulated a number of legislative initiatives, including a massive reorganization of federal administrative functions.

75. The USA PATRIOT Act[76] expanded the categories of terrorism-related inadmissibility and deportation grounds and enhanced law enforcement cooperative efforts. The Enhanced Border Security and Visa Entry Reform Act[77] tightened requirements for visa to the U.S., among other things.

76. The Homeland Security Act, Pub. L. 107–296, 116 Stat. 2135 (2002) enacted the most substantial reorganization of the federal administrative structure since the reforms undertaken under President Franklin Roosevelt under the New Deal of the 1940s. This act created the DHS with a primary mission of combating terrorism. The Homeland Security Act, nonetheless, placed within the DHS a vast array of federal functions, including immigration. The Immigration and Naturalization Service, prior to the Homeland Security Act part of the DOJ, was replaced with bureaus

---

74. Pub. L. 109-162, 119 Statutes-at-Large 2960.
75. Pub. L. 110-457, 122 Statutes-at-Large 5044.
76. Pub. L. 107-56, 115 Statutes-at-Large 272 (2001).
77. Pub. L. 107-173, 116 Statutes-at-Large 543 (2002).

within the DHS, including the Bureau of Customs and Border Protection (CBP), the ICE, and the Bureau of Citizenship and Immigration Services (USCIS). Left within the DOJ was the Executive Office for Immigration Review (EOIR). The EOIR houses the immigration administrative courts: immigration judges and the BIA; thus, the reorganization separated the adjudicatory functions from the prosecutorial and benefit administrative functions.

77. The REAL ID Act[78] provided uniform federal standards for the issuing of driver's licenses, in part, to reduce the likelihood that such a license might be fraudulently used or obtained. In the U.S., driver's licenses are issued by states but are widely accepted for identification purposes by the federal government, including for air travel and most federal functions. The REAL ID Act required states to meet the new federal standards in order for a driver's license to be accepted for federal purposes as adequate identification. The REAL ID Act required that states ascertain the immigration status of applicants for driver's licenses and identification cards; the applicant's status will determine the length of time during which the driver's license or identification card is valid. Thus, most nonimmigrants would receive a temporary driver's license. The provisions of the REAL ID Act represent considerable changes in practice for many states; consequently, states have been granted a number of extensions in implementing the provisions of that Act. As of June 6, 2018, thirty-one states and the District of Columbia are in compliance with the requirements in the Act; nineteen states and the territories of Guam, Northern Mariana Islands, Puerto Rico and the Virgin Islands have been granted a further extension; and only American Samoa, a U.S. territory, is not in compliance. Full enforcement of the REAL ID Act began on February 5, 2018, for territories not in compliance, which would require a U.S. passport, rather than a driver's license for travel and other federal functions. The REAL ID Act also shifted review of federal questions in the context of removal proceedings or orders to federal appellate courts, and further limited judicial review of removal orders.

78. The Secure Fence Act of 2006[79] directed the Secretary of DHS to achieve and maintain operational control of the borders of the U.S. through enhanced surveillance and physical infrastructure enhancements. The enhanced surveillance consisted primarily of technology, including ground-based sensors, satellites, radar coverage, and cameras. The physical infrastructure enhancements consisted of increased checkpoints as well as physical barriers, including the construction of additional reinforced fencing along the U.S.-Mexico border. Currently, CBP maintains approximately 650 miles of fence on the 2,000-mile border between the U.S. and Mexico, leaving around 1,350 miles unfenced. The fencing is designed to stop vehicles, not persons. Only approximately 350 miles of the 2,000-mile border has fencing intended to deter persons from crossing the border.

79. Congress has also enacted a number of statutes to address the needs of a specific population. An example is the Nicaraguan Adjustment and Central American

78. Pub. L. 109-13, 119 Stat. 231 (2005).
79. Pub. L. 109-367, 120 Stat. 2638 (2006).

Relief Act,[80] which granted permanent resident status to a number of Salvadorans, Guatemalans, Nicaraguans and citizens of former Soviet Bloc countries who had been granted TPS in the U.S., who had resided in the U.S. for lengthy periods of time and who were not likely to be able to return to their country of origin in the near future. Haitians caught in the asylum application process for many years were the beneficiaries of the Haitian Refugee Immigration Fairness Act of 1998, Pub. L. 105–227, 112 Statutes-at-Large 2681 (1998). Victims of domestic violence and human trafficking were the beneficiaries of the Violence Against Women and Department of Justice Reauthorization Act of 2005, Pub. L. 109–162, 119 Statutes-at-Large 2960 (2006).

80. Upon entering into office, President Donald Trump issued a series of executive orders suspending the admission of noncitizens from seven Muslim countries, Syrian refugees indefinitely and suspending the U.S. refugee admissions system for a temporary period of time. Some of the provisions were subsequently abandoned or modified and the U.S. Supreme Court ultimately affirmed the authority of the President to suspend admissions from certain countries, because Congress by statute granted the President the discretion to do so and finding that the suspension did not violate the Establishment Clause of the First Amendment because it did not on its face discriminate on the basis of religion. The Biden administration has rescinded entry restrictions on persons from Muslim countries.

81. In January 2017, President Donald Trump signed Executive Order 13767, the Border Security and Immigration Enforcement Improvements Order, directing DHS to expand the use of expedited removal to undocumented immigrants who entered the country without inspection or parole, have been apprehended anywhere in the U.S. and cannot demonstrate that they have been continuously physically present in the U.S. for more than two years. The U.S. Supreme Court recently upheld the application of expedited removal to persons petitioning for asylum reasoning that such persons could not challenge the alleged deprivation of due process through habeas corpus since they were not challenging their detention by the government, the right at the heart of the writ of habeas, but the process through which their application for asylum was determined. The Biden administration has undertaken a review of the expansion of expedited removal.

§3. Overview of International Legal Instruments Applicable in the U.S.

82. The U.S. has ratified a number of conventions that impact immigrant rights, some of which have been the subject of enabling legislation in Congress. The U.S. has ratified the Universal Declaration on Human Rights, December 10, 1948, G.A. Res. 217A (III), generally not treated as creating any express obligations on States/

80. Pub. L. 105-100, 111 Statutes-at-Large 2160 (1997).

Contracting Parties. The U.S. is also bound by the UN Charter, June 26, 1945, TS No. 993, entered into force October 24, 1945, as one of the UN's founding members.

83. The Convention Relating to the Status of Refugees, July 28, 1951, 189 UNTS 137 (1951 UN Refugee Convention) and the Protocol Relating to the Status of Refugees, January 31, 1967, 606 UNTS 267, entered into force October 4, 1967 (1967 Protocol), as well as the Convention Against Torture and Other Cruel, Inhuman or Degrading Treatment of Punishment, December 10, 1984, 1465 UNTS 85, entered into force June 26, 1987, (the Convention Against Torture) have been incorporated into U.S. law through the 1980 Refugee Act. The U.S. is not a party to the 1951 UN Refugee Convention, but is a party to the 1967 Protocol, which incorporates Articles 2–34 of the 1951 UN Refugee Convention. Under the 1951 UN Refugee Convention and its 1967 Protocol, States are required to grant refugees benefits like authorization to work, access to courts, and freedom of movement, the kind of rights or benefits that USCs and LPRs enjoy. The 1951 Refugee Convention does not require that States admit refugees but prohibits States from returning a refugee to a country where she/he would face persecution or threats to her/his life or freedom, the principle known as non-refoulement under international law. For the purpose of the 1951 UN Refugee Convention and U.S. immigration law, a refugee is defined as a person who, owing to persecution or a well-founded fear of being persecuted for reasons of race, religion, nationality, membership in a particular social group, or political opinion, is outside the country of his nationality and is unable or, owing to such fear, is unwilling to avail himself of the protection of that country.

84. The U.S. has also ratified the International Covenant on Civil and Political Rights, December 16, 1966, 999 UNTS 171, entered into force on March 23, 1976, and ratified by the U.S. on September 8, 1992 and the International Convention on the Elimination of All Forms of Racial Discrimination, December 21, 1965, 660 UNTS 195, entered into force on January 4, 1969, and ratified by the U.S. on November 20, 1994.

85. The U.S. has ratified the Vienna Convention on Diplomatic Relations, April 18, 1961, 500 UNTS 95, entered into force April 24, 1964, and the Vienna Convention on Consular Relations, April 24, 1963, 596 UNTS 261, entered into force March 19, 1967. The U.S. has also ratified the Optional Protocol Concerning the Settlement of Disputes arising from the Vienna Convention on Consular Relations, subjecting the U.S. to the compulsory jurisdiction of the International Court of Justice (ICJ) for dispute resolution. The Convention on Consular Relations requires Contracting Parties to inform noncitizens who are arrested or detained of their right to contact consular officials upon arrest or detention. The U.S. has had difficulties in implementing these obligations, in part, because arresting authorities in many cases involving criminal activity are U.S. state authorities. Congress has never passed express enabling legislation requiring the states to comply with these obligations, and some states in the U.S. have refused to comply. The issue recently reached the U.S. Supreme Court.

86. In the Case Concerning Avena and Other Mexican Nationals (*Mex. v. U.S.*),[81] the ICJ held that individuals subject to criminal process and on death row in the U.S. but denied access to their consuls upon arrest were entitled to review and reconsider their U.S. state court conviction regardless of the individual state's own prohibition against filing successive habeas petitions, which ordinarily prohibited further review of the underlying conviction. In *Sanchez-Llamas v. Oregon*,[82] a case involving defendants like those before the ICJ but not the specific individuals in the Avena case, the U.S. Supreme Court essentially disagreed with the ICJ and held that state rules limiting successive habeas petitions applied to bar further review of convictions. Consequently, the President issued a memorandum that the U.S. would discharge its international obligations under Article 36(1)(b) of the Vienna Convention on Consular Relations by having state courts give effect to the Avena decision. The President's memorandum was a unilateral act, unsupported by Congressional legislation or resolution. In February 2005, the U.S. also withdrew from the Optional Protocol Concerning the Settlement of Disputes. In the case of *Medellin v. Texas*,[83] the Supreme Court held that the ICJ's Avena judgment was not a directly enforceable federal law that would preempt state limits on the filing of successive habeas petitions, unless Congress passed a statute giving effect to the judgment. The Supreme Court held that the Vienna Convention on Consular Relations was not self-executing and held further that the President lacked inherent power to order state courts to give effect to the Avena judgment. Mr. Medellin, subsequently, was executed by the state of Texas on August 5, 2008.

87. The North American Free Trade Agreement (NAFTA), adopted on December 17, 1992, 32 ILM 605, entered into force on January 1, 1994, an agreement creating special trade relationships between Canada, Mexico and the U.S., grants preferential treatment for business persons and highly skilled workers for temporary entry into their countries, including the U.S. The agreement does not provide for free movement of labor between the countries. In May 2017, the President informed Congress that he was commencing negotiations with Canada and Mexico concerning NAFTA. The new US-Mexico-Canada Agreement went into effect on July 1, 2020. The provisions of the new agreement appear not to differ greatly from NAFTA with regards to trade, but the new agreement specifically addresses the protection of workers, including migrant workers, an issue that had not been addressed by the original NAFTA. The new agreement commits the three parties to recognition of the right of association and collective bargaining, the abolition of child labor and the prohibition against gender discrimination in employment. The parties expressly recognize "that it is inappropriate to encourage trade or investment by weakening or reducing the protections afforded in each Party's labor laws." Under the new agreement, Mexico has agreed to pass laws giving workers the right to union representation, to extend labor protection to migrant workers, and to protect women from discrimination. The three countries commit to ensuring that "migrant

81. 2004 I.C.J. 12 (Avena).
82. 548 U.S. 331 (2006).
83. 552 U.S. 491 (2008).

workers are protected under its labor laws, whether they are nationals or non-nationals of the Party." With regards to the protection of workers against discrimination on the basis of sex, the agreement specifically includes sexual harassment and discrimination on the basis of pregnancy, sexual orientation, gender identity, and caregiving responsibilities, to some extent expanding the protection currently available in some parts of the U.S. The agreement also allows each country to sanction the others for labor violations that impact trade. In addition, 40% of cars assembled in Mexico by U.S. auto companies have to be made by workers earning at least USD 16 an hour, three times more than Mexico's minimum wage for an entire workday. The agreement addresses temporary admissions for business-related visitors in a wide range of professions and business activities, well within the range of current U.S. temporary worker or visitor visa categories. The new agreement also contains provisions concerning environmental protection, another area that had been left out of the original NAFTA.

88. The U.S. signed the Hague Convention on Protection of Children and Co-operation with Respect to Intercountry Adoption in 1994 and it entered into force for the U.S. in April 2008. The Convention regulates intercountry adoptions between the U.S. and other Convention countries.

89. The U.S. has signed but not yet ratified the Convention on the Elimination of All Forms of Discrimination Against Women (CEDAW), UNGA Res. 34/180 UN Dec A/Res/34/180 (1980). Notwithstanding its failure to ratify CEDAW, the U.S., through its domestic laws, provides a high level of protection against discrimination on the basis of gender, and generally makes available both public and private mechanisms for enforcement of anti-discrimination gender norms.

90. The U.S. has signed and ratified the Convention against Transnational Organized Crime and Protocols Thereto (Convention on Human Trafficking), ratified by the U.S. on November 3, 2005, adopted by the UN General Assembly on November 15, 2000, entered into force on September 29, 2003.

Part I. Border Control and Entrance

Chapter 1. Organization of Border Control

91. The power to regulate and implement immigration laws is exercised by three cabinet-level departments: the DHS, within which the primary agencies implementing immigration authority are housed; the DOS, with primary authority for the issuance of visa for travel to the U.S.; and the DOJ, with primary federal law enforcement authority in the U.S., including federal criminal statutory violations, and housing administrative immigration courts that decide deportation and removal cases.

92. The primary federal agency responsible for overseeing control of the borders of the U.S. is the Bureau of CBP, part of the U.S. DHS. CBP's mission is to check terrorism, human smuggling, drug smuggling, weapons smuggling, and irregular migration along the U.S. borders, including at official points of entry, like international airports, seaports and land border checkpoints. CBP is responsible for conducting inspections of individuals and cargo, and overseeing entries at authorized entry points. The Border Patrol, part of the CBP, oversees the rest of the border area to prevent and apprehend unauthorized entrants.

93. The ICE, also part of DHS, has primary authority for investigating customs and immigration law violations within the U.S. ICE conducts investigations, arrests, detentions, deportations, and exercises the prosecutorial function in civil administrative immigration-related proceedings, like removals. ICE is also responsible for the enforcement of laws prohibiting unauthorized employment of noncitizens. ICE also investigates human trafficking.

94. The USCIS administers immigrant benefits, including immigrant visa, work authorization or adjustments of status, and naturalizations. USCIS is the agency where the permanent visa process begins because most visas for permanent residence in the U.S. are granted on the basis of a family relationship with a USC or LPR, or on the basis of an employment relationship with a U.S. employer. A visa request must be initiated by the USC, LPR, or employer in the U.S. and filed with the USCIS. A specialized branch of USCIS is responsible for the processing of asylum applications. USCIS is also the agency that decides on applications for visa extensions or adjustments.

95. The DOS, however, has primary authority to issue and deny visas. The Bureau of Consular Affairs has responsibility for visa issuance. Most nonimmigrant visas, such as tourist or business visitor visas, may be initiated by the visa petitioner through the DOS consular officer in the petitioner's home country. For visas that require a U.S. entity, USC or LPR petitioner, once a petitioner has filed a visa petition with USCIS, the visa will be processed, approved and issued through the State Department's Consular Office in the visa beneficiary's home country, but with significant interaction with the USCIS.

96. The DOJ houses the EOIR, the system of immigration administrative courts whose prime function is to hear and decide on removal and relief from removal cases. EOIR consists of Immigration Courts, the administrative courts that exercise a fact-finding function, and the BIA, the administrative appellate board that reviews immigration judge's decisions. Currently, there are approximately 400 immigration judges throughout the U.S., many of them located in federal detention facilities. Currently, the BIA is composed of fifteen permanent judges (it may seat up to twenty-one judges), who have the power to summarily affirm immigration judge's decisions individually in certain cases, but who may also sit in panels of three to review immigration judge's decisions. The BIA has jurisdiction to hear appeals from decisions of immigration judges and district directors of DHS in a variety of proceedings, including fines imposed on carriers for violation of immigration laws and petitions to classify the status of noncitizen relatives for the issuance of preference immigrant visa. Immigration courts, including the BIA, exercise the discretion of the Attorney General of the U.S.; as a result, the Attorney General retains the discretion to take cases from the BIA and decide them instead. The Attorney General has seldom exercised this discretion. However, the Attorney General recently exercised this discretion in a number of matters, in particular dealing with asylum. The Attorney General's reinterpretation of asylum law has restricted the granting of asylum in cases involving gender-motivated violence and gang violence. Federal appellate courts exercise review over federal questions, including statutory interpretation and constitutional issues that arise in removal cases, but exercise limited review over the actual decision whether to remove a noncitizen or not, or over discretionary relief decisions, for instance whether a particular noncitizen is entitled to relief from removal.

97. The DOL, another cabinet-level department, plays a role in the issuance of employment-based visas, both for visas for permanent residence and visas for short-stay residence. Many employment-based visas require a finding by the DOL that issuance of an employment visa will not adversely affect the conditions and wages of workers in the U.S., and that there are no able and willing U.S. workers available to fill the position. For the purposes of labor certification, U.S. workers are U.S. citizens, nationals, persons lawfully admitted for permanent residence, refugees and asylees. Employers may appeal denials of labor certification to the Board of Alien Labor Certification Appeals.

98. The Public Health Service, an agency in the Department of Health and Human Services headed by the Surgeon General, exercises some authority over the medical or health-related inadmissibility grounds and also provides any medical examination that may be required of visa applicants prior to admission.

Chapter 2. Right to Enter the Country

99. As a general matter, U.S. law does not recognize a right of entry for noncitizens. Noncitizens wishing to be admitted to the U.S. must petition for permission to enter the country. Permission is granted in the form of a visa and that visa must be issued prior to the noncitizens presenting themselves at an authorized point of entry. Even with a properly issued visa by the DOS, the U.S. retains the authority to deny admission to individual noncitizens at the point of entry; thus, a second inspection and visa determination occur at the point of entry. In most cases, noncitizens with a valid passport and valid visa at the point of entry proceed to enter without difficulty. To secure admission into the U.S., therefore, a valid unexpired passport and a valid visa must be presented. The only exception to this rule is when a person requests asylum, as more fully explained in the section on asylum below.[84] Simply asking for asylum will not secure admission to the U.S., without a valid passport and visa, and even a person who convinces an immigration official at a point of entry that she/he has a legitimate claim for asylum may be subject to detention in the U.S. until their claim has been administratively adjudicated. The Trump administration made it more difficult for asylum seekers presenting themselves at the U.S.-Mexico border to actually enter the U.S. to apply for asylum, insisting instead that asylum seekers return to or remain in Mexico while their claims are considered in a removal proceeding. The Migrant Protection Protocols (MPP) issued on January 25, 2019, did not apply to unaccompanied noncitizen children, Mexican citizens, persons placed in expedited removal, returning LPRs seeking admission, persons who are more likely than not to face persecution or torture in Mexico, and other noncitizens at the discretion of the Port Director. The MPP, however, applied to most noncitizens who are not Mexican citizens seeking to apply for asylum at the U.S.-Mexico border. On February 11, 2021, the Biden administration announced that it would process eligible persons forced to remain in Mexico due to the MPP in the U.S. Currently, the change in policy will affect approximately 25,000 persons.

100. Generally, noncitizens who previously have been admitted to the U.S. as immigrants, that is, as permanent residents, have a limited right to reentry, as more thoroughly explained below. Only citizens, however, enjoy a fully protected right of entry, lost only upon renunciation of citizenship.

101. Noncitizens seeking admission to the U.S. are divided into two basic groups under U.S. immigration law: immigrants, those noncitizens intending to permanently reside and work in the U.S.; and nonimmigrants, defined in the INA by categories which include persons coming to the U.S. for short stays, and persons who are coming to the U.S. to engage in temporary work, or to undertake lengthy courses of study.[85] Under the INA, any noncitizen who does not fall within one of the statutorily defined classes of nonimmigrants is presumed to be an immigrant.[86]

84. 8 U.S.C. §1181(c).
85. 8 U.S.C. §1101(a)(15).
86. 8 U.S.C. §1184(b).

102. Noncitizens who have been admitted to permanent residency are on the path to citizenship through naturalization. U.S. law does not require that permanent residents become citizens of the U.S. to continue to reside in the U.S., and many permanent residents choose not to pursue U.S. citizenship. However, as permanent residents they remain vulnerable to deportation. Currently, in order to naturalize an immigrant must be at least 18 years of age; have resided in the U.S. continuously for five years; be able to speak, read and write English; demonstrate knowledge of the history and government of the U.S.; and be of good moral character. Some elderly persons may be excused from the English fluency requirement. As the grounds that render a permanent resident noncitizen deportable have expanded, the rate of naturalization petitions has increased. In addition, USCIS, the agency charged with processing naturalization applications has made an effort to reduce processing delays that force an applicant to wait for longer than five years to become a citizen. Spouses of U.S. citizens are eligible for naturalization after three years and noncitizens who serve in the military may be eligible for fast-track naturalization as well. Adult permanent residents, with minor children at the time they file their application for naturalization, may include their minor children in their naturalization petition. In 2009, 743,715 persons naturalized; in 2010 the number of naturalizations decreased to 619,913; in 2011, approximately 694,193 LPRs naturalized; in 2012, approximately 757,434 LPRs naturalized; and in 2013, approximately 779,929 LPRs naturalized. Naturalizations dropped again in 2014, with a total of 653,416 naturalizations that year. In 2015, 730,259 LPRs naturalized; in 2016, 753,060 LPRs naturalized and in 2017, 707,265 LPRs naturalized. In 2018, 761,901 persons naturalized.

103. The leading region of origin of new U.S. citizens in most years since 1976 has been Asia. For the first time since 1976, in 2017 and 2018, the North American region led the number of naturalizations but only slightly. The leading regions of origin of persons naturalizing in 2017 and 2018 were North American (258,371 and 277,592, respectively) and Asian (255,306 and 275,621, respectively). The leading country of birth of persons naturalizing in 2017 was Mexico, with 118,559 naturalizations and 131,977 naturalizations in 2018; followed by India, with 50,802 in 2017 and 52,194 in 2018; the People's Republic of China, with 37,674 naturalizations in 2017 and 39,600 in 2018; the Philippines, with 36,828 naturalizations in 2017 and 38,816 in 2018. In 2017, the Dominican Republic followed with 29,734 naturalizations, but in 2018 Cuba's naturalization numbers placed it ahead of the Dominican Republic: naturalizations of Cuban permanent residents rose to 32,089, whereas Dominican Republic naturalizations numbered 22,970. The median amount of time spent in LPR status for persons who naturalized in 2013 was seven years. The majority of persons naturalizing (56%) that year were women, and a half (50%) of new citizens were between the ages of 25 and 44. The majority of persons naturalizing in 2017 were married (64%). In 2018, the majority of persons naturalizing were women and for both men and women, the majority were married.

104. Most nonimmigrant categories are not subject to a numerical cap with the exception of temporary workers. Moreover, nonimmigrant categories are subject to the same inadmissibility grounds that apply to immigrants. Nonimmigrant categories, however, may be eligible for waivers from the inadmissibility grounds that may not be available to immigrants.

§1. Conditions for Entry: Temporary Visitors for Business or Pleasure

105. Most nonimmigrant admissions to the U.S. are tourists—visitors for pleasure. Generally, the conditions for entry as a nonimmigrant are that the noncitizens have a residence in a foreign country that she or he has no intention of abandoning, and that the visit is temporary for either business purposes or pleasure. Temporary visitors for business or pleasure generally will have to demonstrate sufficient financial resources to maintain themselves during their visit to the U.S. and to return to their home country.

106. Tourists who are nationals of certain countries and seek admission for only ninety days may seek admission through the visa waiver program. To be eligible for admission through the visa waiver program, the noncitizen must have a round trip ticket; must have a machine-readable passport; must not have violated the terms of any previous admission to the U.S.; and must waive any rights to appeal a negative admission determination.[87]

107. Tourists, temporary visitors for pleasure, generally are granted a six-month period of admission through a B-2 visa. Tourists are not authorized to work in the U.S. Persons who enter with a visitor for pleasure visa may apply to extend their visit to the U.S., unless they entered through the visa waiver program.

108. Temporary visitors for business similarly are granted a six-month to one-year period of admission through the B-1 visa. The B-1 visa is not available for noncitizens who are paid a salary or wage by a U.S.-based company. Thus, the visa is envisioned as a mechanism through which persons who are self-employed or employed by a non-U.S.-based company may enter the U.S. to attend conferences, conduct research, deliver or attend lectures, enter into business dealings and other similar types of engagements for non-U.S.-based companies. Persons entering on a B-1 visa may have their incidental expenses paid for by a U.S.-based entity and may receive an honorarium for speaking at a conference from a U.S.-based entity, but the number of events and the length of time of their stay may be restricted. B-1 visa holders may apply to extend the length of their stay to USCIS.

§2. Administrative Procedures and Documents for Entry

109. Nonimmigrants seeking admission to the U.S. are required to apply for a visa at a U.S. consulate overseas. To apply for a visitor for pleasure visa or business

87. 8 U.S.C. §1187.

visa, the applicant must file DOS Form 160. The filing fee for Form 160 is USD 160. In certain circumstances, the applicants may be required to submit supporting documentation to establish that they are not intending immigrants and that they have the resources to travel to the U.S. and return to their country of origin. The consular office, under the DOS, will issue a visa that authorizes the noncitizens to travel to the U.S. and present themselves for admission at a point of entry. Immigration officials at the point of entry in the U.S. will consider the noncitizen for admission; if the documents are not in order or the individual poses a security risk, she/he will be denied entry. Thus, having been issued a visa does not entitle one to entry. Prior to entry at land border ports of entry, a noncitizen will be asked to fill out an I-94, a form that is issued at the point of entry, which constitutes authorization to be in the U.S. for the specified period of time. CBP has streamlined the admissions process for foreign visitors arriving by sea or air and electronically gathers the information from the travelers' electronic travel records. At the port of entry, CBP stamps a traveler's passport with the date of admission, the admission category and an "admitted until" date. Travelers who do not have the paper I-94 Form will be able to access their information electronically.

110. Some nonimmigrants may be entitled to enter without a visa through the visa waiver program. Under the visa waiver program, nonimmigrants from a number of countries are entitled to entry for a period of ninety days as tourists or business visitors without applying for a visa.[88] Persons entering under the visa waiver program simply have to present a valid passport issued by one of the visa waiver program countries. Currently, persons wishing to enter through the visa waiver program are required to submit before travel the Electronic System for Travel Authorization (ESTA) to the CBP in the DHS. An ESTA is valid for up to two years or until the passport expires, whichever comes first, and may be used to enter the U.S. for ninety-day periods on multiple occasions. The filing fee for ESTA is USD 4 for the processing charge and an additional USD 10 authorization charge if the application is approved. As of June 2015, there are thirty-eight countries in the visa waiver program, including Australia, New Zealand, Japan and Iceland.

111. Nonimmigrants who have been admitted to the U.S. under one nonimmigrant category may apply to have their status adjusted to another category with the USCIS.

88. *Ibid.*

Chapter 3. Refusal of Entry: Inadmissibility

112. The INA provides the classes of noncitizens who are ineligible for a visa or admission to the U.S. in §1182 of Title 8 of the U.S.C. The main grounds that render a person inadmissible reflect concerns over personal health including infectious diseases; criminal activity; national security concerns; public charge concerns; and immigration-related concerns like unauthorized entry. Some of the inadmissibility grounds are waivable and some are not. Some are waivable for persons who are seeking admission as nonimmigrants, but not for persons seeking admission as immigrants.

113. The inadmissibility grounds apply to persons applying for a visa, and to persons applying for admission to the U.S.[89] Whether a noncitizen is considered "admitted" or seeking "admission" to the U.S. is defined in the INA. Thus, "admission" and "admitted" mean "the lawful entry of the alien into the United States after inspection and authorization by an immigration officer."[90] Persons who are paroled into the U.S. are not considered admitted to the U.S., although they may reside in the U.S. for many years, or are foreign crewmen permitted to land temporarily.

114. Permanent residents who travel abroad generally are not regarded as seeking admission to the U.S. upon their return unless one of the following conditions apply:

- the noncitizen has abandoned or relinquished her or his status;
- the noncitizen has been absent from the U.S. for a continuous period in excess of six months;
- the noncitizen has engaged in an illegal activity after having departed from the U.S.;
- the noncitizen departed from the U.S. while in removal proceedings in the U.S.;
- the noncitizen has committed certain criminal offenses; or
- the noncitizen attempts unauthorized entry.[91]

115. The category of inadmissibility that focuses on health-related grounds provides that noncitizens who have a communicable disease of public health significance are inadmissible. In addition, noncitizens who are seeking admission as immigrants must provide documentation of vaccination for a number of vaccine-preventable diseases, like mumps, measles, rubella, polio, tetanus and other diseases. Also, certain physical or mental disorders which pose threats to property, safety or welfare of the noncitizen or others may render that person inadmissible. Finally, the statute makes drug abuse or addiction a ground of inadmissibility. Children younger than 10 are exempted from some of the vaccination requirements. Most of the health-related grounds are waivable for certain categories of applicants

89. 8 U.S.C. §1182.
90. 8 U.S.C. §1101(a)(13)(A).
91. 8 U.S.C. §1101(a)(13)(A)(C).

or with certain conditions, including providing a bond in certain circumstances.[92] In addition, most of the inadmissibility grounds, including the public health grounds, are waivable for nonimmigrants who are seeking temporary admission.[93]

116. The INA gives the Secretary of Health and Human Services primary responsibility for promulgating regulations dealing with the health-related grounds.

117. One of the major categories to render a substantial number of noncitizens inadmissible to the U.S. concerns criminal-related grounds.[94] The criminal grounds involve application of federal criminal law, the criminal law of the fifty states, and to some extent foreign criminal law. Each individual state has its own set of criminal statutes, so the application of the inadmissibility criminal grounds, when the subject of litigation, can be complex and requires legal research into state and federal criminal law. Generally, criminal convictions will render a noncitizen ineligible for admission into the U.S. However, the criminal-related grounds do not require an actual conviction; simply committing acts that constitute the essential elements of the described offenses will render a person inadmissible. The criminal-related grounds revolve around crimes involving moral turpitude, as defined under U.S. immigration law, including attempts or conspiracies to commit such crimes; or violation of any federal or state law concerning controlled substances. The statute creates narrow exceptions for a single offense involving moral turpitude, committed as a minor, if the offense was committed more than five years before the date of application; or if the sentence imposed was minimal (less than six months imprisonment) and the maximum sentence for the offense is less than one year.

118. Controlled substances offenses include drug trafficking offenses and those provisions render family members of traffickers inadmissible if they have obtained any financial or other benefit from the illicit activity, or if they knew or reasonably should have known that the benefit was the product of the illicit activity.[95]

119. The only exception to inadmissibility for offenses involving controlled substances is for a single offense of simple possession of 30 grams or less of marijuana if the immigrant is the spouse, parent, son or daughter of a citizen or lawful permanent resident of the U.S. and the Attorney General determines that the immigrant's denial of admission would result in extreme hardship to the USC or permanent resident spouse, parent, son, or daughter of such immigrant or if the immigrant is a VAWA self-petitioner and the Attorney General consents to the waiver. Most of the other criminal-related grounds, including prostitution and gambling, are eligible for the waiver from inadmissibility. Serious offenses, like murder, torture, human trafficking, money laundering and aggravated felonies (as defined for the purpose of U.S. immigration law), are not waivable. In cases involving permanent residents, the statute requires that for the waiver to be available the permanent

92. 8 U.S.C. §1182(g).
93. 8 U.S.C. §1182(d).
94. 8 U.S.C. §1182(a)(2).
95. 8 U.S.C. §1182(a)(2)(C).

resident must have resided in the U.S. for a period of seven years immediately preceding the date of initiation of removal proceedings. Whether a particular noncitizen receives a waiver or not is generally not subject to judicial review.[96]

120. Another category that has substantial impact on admissions is the national security grounds.[97] These grounds do not require convictions or commission of any affirmative acts; instead, the INA vests substantial discretion in consular officers to declare inadmissible any alien who the consular officer (or DHS official) "know[s], or has reasonable ground to believe" seeks to enter the U.S. to engage in any activity related to espionage, sabotage, terrorism or any other unlawful activity. Moreover, the INA mandates that any alien, who has engaged in, endorsed or espoused terrorist activity, broadly defined, is inadmissible. Immediate family members of persons who fall in this category are similarly inadmissible if the activity occurred within the last five years. The only exception is provided for family members who did not know or should not have reasonably known of the activity, or whom the consular officer has reasonable grounds to believe have renounced the activity. Engaging in terrorist activities includes soliciting funds or other things of value for a terrorist organization or to provide material support to a terrorist organization, in addition to planning, carrying out, or inciting in terrorist activities. Terrorist organizations are those organizations designated by the Secretary of State in consultation with the Attorney General or the Secretary of Homeland Security and published in the Federal Register; an organization designated pursuant to 8 U.S.C. §1189; or an organization (a group of two or more individuals), which engages in terrorist activity. Any alien who associates with a terrorist organization and intends to engage in activities while in the U.S. "that could endanger the welfare, safety, or security of the United States is inadmissible."[98]

121. Also within national security concerns is a category reflecting foreign policy grounds for inadmissibility. The foreign policy grounds authorize the Secretary of State to declare an alien inadmissible if the Secretary of State "has reasonable ground to believe" that the alien's entry or proposed activities in the U.S. "would have potentially serious adverse foreign policy consequences for the United States."[99] The INA vests discretion in the Secretary of State to make certain exceptions in certain cases, particularly cases that reflect tensions with freedoms that under the First Amendment to the U.S. Constitution receive a high level of protection from government interference. The national security grounds continue to render a current or past member of the Communist Party or any other totalitarian party inadmissible,[100] as well as aliens who participated in Nazi persecutions.[101]

96. 8 U.S.C. §1182(h).
97. 8 U.S.C. §1182(a)(3).
98. 8 U.S.C. §1182(a)(3)(F).
99. 8 U.S.C. §1182(a)(3)(C).
100. 8 U.S.C. §1182(a)(3)(D).
101. 8 U.S.C. §1182(a)(3)(E).

122. The INA also prohibits the admission of aliens who ordered, incited, assisted, or otherwise participated in genocide, torture or extrajudicial killings.[102]

123. The INA declares any alien likely to become a public charge inadmissible. In determining whether to declare someone inadmissible because she or he is likely to become a public charge, the consular officer shall consider that person's age, health, family status, assets, resources, financial status, education and skills. Family-sponsored immigrants are inadmissible unless the person petitioning for the immigrant's admission provides an affidavit of support that guarantees financial support of the visa beneficiary. An exception is available for spouses and children of USCs. Some employment-based immigrant visa also require affidavits of support.[103]

124. As a general matter, any alien who is present without having been admitted or paroled into the U.S. or who entered the U.S. without inspection is inadmissible.[104] Exceptions to this rule are provided for aliens who have been the victims of domestic or intimate battering or violence. In addition, failing to attend a removal proceeding, or misrepresentation of any material fact in securing a visa, other document or admission to the U.S., will render an alien inadmissible. Similarly, any alien who has knowingly encouraged, induced, assisted, abetted, or aided any other alien to enter or to try to enter the U.S. without inspection or in violation of law is inadmissible. Limited waivers in narrow circumstances are provided for some of these categories of inadmissibility.

125. Immigrants who are permanently ineligible for citizenship are inadmissible. Immigrants who remain outside the U.S. to avoid or evade service in the armed forces in time of war or at a time of national emergency are also inadmissible.[105]

126. The INA also contains bars to admission for aliens who have previously been removed by order from the U.S. An alien who has been removed by order from the U.S. is inadmissible for five years after the date of removal. For some aliens the period of inadmissibility is ten years. In cases involving aliens who have been removed by order more than once, the period of inadmissibility is twenty years. The INA provides for a discretionary waiver from these bars to admissibility.[106] The statute provides an additional three year (unlawfully present for longer than six months but less than one year) or ten year (unlawfully present for longer than one year) bars for most aliens unlawfully present in the U.S. The statute provides limited exceptions to these bars and provides a discretionary waiver from the bars for an immigrant who is the spouse or son or daughter of a USC or lawful permanent residence

102. *Ibid.*
103. 8 U.S.C. §1182(a)(4).
104. 8 U.S.C. §1182(a)(6).
105. 8 U.S.C. §1182(a)(8).
106. 8 U.S.C. §1182(a)(9).

if refusal of admission to the immigrant would result in extreme hardship to the citizen or lawfully resident spouse or parent of such immigrant.[107]

127. The INA provides additional miscellaneous grounds that render a noncitizen inadmissible to the U.S. which include practicing polygamy, abducting children, voting unlawfully (voting in a federal, state or local election as a noncitizen where such voting is not authorized by law), and renouncing citizenship to avoid paying federal taxes.[108]

107. 8 U.S.C. §1182(a)(9)(B)(v).
108. 8 U.S.C. §1182(a)(10).

Part II. Right of Residence: General Provisions

Chapter 1. Short Stay: Nonimmigrants—Visa Waiver Program; B-1 Business Visitors and B-2 Visitors for Pleasure

128. U.S. immigration law distinguishes between immigrants, those noncitizens admitted to permanent residence in the U.S., and nonimmigrants, those noncitizens admitted for a temporary period of time and for a specific purpose (tourism, business, temporary work, education, or research). The INA describes the various nonimmigrant categories that are referred to by their visa designation; for example, B-1 visa for temporary business visitors and B-2 visa for temporary pleasure visitors. The visa designations come directly from the INA sections describing the particular visa.

129. For the purpose of this monograph, short stay nonimmigrants include noncitizens entering under the visa waiver program, admitted for a period of ninety days; tourists or temporary visitors for pleasure, admitted for a period of six months; and temporary visitors for business, admitted for a period of six months to one year.

§1. Conditions for Short Stay

130. To enter under the visa waiver program, a noncitizen must reside in and have a valid passport issued by a country that is recognized in the visa waiver program. In addition, the noncitizen must not fall within one of the inadmissibility grounds. Generally, a passport must be valid for six months beyond the termination of the period of stay. The passport must be machine-readable and must contain a digital photograph and an e-chip (a small-integrated computer chip embedded in the back cover which stores information, including a biometric identifier, a unique chip identification number and a digital signature).

§2. Administrative Procedures and Documents for Short Stay

131. To enter under the visa waiver program, the nonimmigrant must obtain a valid ESTA approval before travel. If the nonimmigrant is found to be inadmissible

Chapter 2. Residence: Nonimmigrants

§1. Conditions of Residence

139. As explained above, the conditions of residence for nonimmigrants, noncitizens who are admitted to the U.S. for a specific purpose and a temporary, generally fixed period of time are determined by the terms of their specific visa. Generally, nonimmigrants must intend to return to their home country at the time that they apply for their nonimmigrant visa; they must have a place of residence abroad that they have no intention of abandoning; and they must have sufficient resources to accommodate their visit to the U.S. and return to their home country.

§2. Administrative Procedures and Documents for Residence for Nonimmigrants

140. Most nonimmigrants will apply for their visa to the U.S. consulate in their home country. Some nonimmigrant visa, however, require filings with USCIS and completion of the labor certification process through the DOL. Nonimmigrants will complete and file with the U.S. consular office in the district in which they reside a Form DS-160, the nonimmigrant visa application form, with any supporting documents that are necessary to establish eligibility for the visa. Noncitizens generally also must submit digital photographs and the application fee (USD 160 or USD 190 for petition-based visas). Some nonimmigrants may be required to provide a police certificate or clearance. Other documentation required for specific visa categories, like USCIS approval, DOL labor certification or attestation, or the Student and Exchange Visitor Information System (SEVIS) certificate and SEVIS fee (for student visa categories) must be submitted as well. Each family member accompanying the visa holder must submit a separate nonimmigrant visa application. Generally, all applicants will appear for a personal interview with a consular officer, although interviews may be waived for children under 14 years of age or persons over 79 years of age, diplomats, or if it is in the national interest or if there are unusual circumstances that justify waiving the personal interview. Nonimmigrants will generally be fingerprinted and photographed at the consular office to facilitate the issuance of machine-readable, tamper-resistant travel documents containing biometric identifiers. Visa processing may take time due to enhanced security processes.

§3. Legal Position of Nonimmigrants

141. After admission, nonimmigrants must abide by the terms of their visa. Violation of the conditions of their visa renders a nonimmigrant removable. Nonimmigrants are subject to federal and state laws. Generally, nonimmigrants are entitled to the same protection that USCs and LPRs receive in criminal process. In removal proceedings they enjoy the same procedural safeguards as LPRs.

§4. Position of Family Members of Nonimmigrants

142. Family members of nonimmigrants who accompany or follow to join may be limited in employment and in pursuing public education depending on the terms of the nonimmigrant visa category they are admitted under.

Chapter 3. Long-Term Residence: Immigrants

143. The U.S. makes available annually at least 600,000 visas to immigrants—persons intending to take up permanent residence in the U.S. Immigrant visa to the U.S. are based on particular family relationships to a citizen or permanent resident noncitizen of the U.S. and on an employment relationship with a U.S. employer. In addition, the INA provides 50,000 visas annually to diversity immigrants and to employment creation immigrants. Employment-based immigrant categories will be discussed in Part VII, Access to the Labor Market section of this monograph, as will the employment creation immigrant category. Diversity immigrants are discussed in Part III, Right of Residence for Special Categories of Persons, Chapter 7, Others. As described below, the INA specifies the family and employment relationships that will render a noncitizen eligible for an immigrant visa. Persons admitted for permanent residence generally enjoy all benefits and rights that USCs enjoy, with the exception of the franchise, and access to welfare or food stamps. Permanent residents, however, remain vulnerable to removal until they become citizens.

§1. Conditions for Long-Term Right of Residence: Family-Based Admission Categories

I. Immediate Relatives of USCs

144. Under the INA, immediate relatives of USCs means the children, spouse and parents of a citizen of the U.S., except that in the case of parents, the citizen must be at least 21 years of age in order for the parent to be eligible for an immigrant visa.[109] Immediate relatives of USCs are not subject to direct numerical limitations. This means that they do not have to wait until a visa becomes available but will be eligible for admission as soon as their petition is approved.

145. The term "child" is statutorily defined in the INA and includes primarily an unmarried person under 21 years of age.[110] Stepchildren are included if the child has not reached the age of 18 years at the time of the marriage creating the status of stepchild. Non-marital children are included if legitimated before the child reaches the age of 18 years and the child is in the legal custody of the legitimating parent or parents at the time of the legitimation. Adopted children are included as well if adopted while under the age of 16 years.

146. For the purpose of the INA, the term "spouse" does not include a spouse, wife or husband by reason of a marriage ceremony where the contracting parties are not physically present at the ceremony, unless the marriage is consummated.[111] Marriage by proxy, therefore, does not suffice to vest the immigration benefit on a

109. 8 U.S.C. §1151(b)(2)(A)(i).
110. 8 U.S.C. §1101(b)(1).
111. 8 U.S.C. §1101(35).

spouse. Courts have interpreted the INA to require that for a person to qualify as a spouse the marriage must be valid under state law and under federal immigration law. To be a valid marriage for immigration purposes, at a minimum, the marriage must be a real marriage and it must not have been entered into for the purpose of deriving a benefit under U.S. immigration law. U.S. immigration law deems marriages entered into for the purpose of procuring an alien's admission as an immigrant a fraudulent marriage.[112] The U.S. recognizes same-sex marriages as qualifying marriages including for the purpose of immigration benefits. All rules that apply to a heterosexual marriage apply to same-sex marriage.

147. Moreover, spouses who have entered into a marriage creating an immigration benefit through a marriage that is less than two years old are admitted as permanent residents on a conditional basis.[113] If during the two years, the marriage is annulled or terminated other than by the spouse's death, or if the DHS determines that the marriage was fraudulent, the foreigner's permanent resident status is terminated and removal hearings will be instigated. At the removal hearing the burden of proof will be on the government.

148. At the end of two years, the conditional resident and the spouse have an affirmative duty to jointly petition for removal of the condition and to appear at an interview to adjudicate the petition.[114] Failure to file a timely petition (during the ninety-day period before the second anniversary of the alien's obtaining the status of lawful admission for permanent residence) will be the cause for terminating the alien's permanent resident status. If the petition is filed timely, the couple appear for the interview and USCIS determines that the marriage was legally valid, that it has not been annulled or terminated, that it was not entered into to secure the immigration benefit and that no fee was paid to anyone (other than to an attorney) for the filing of the petition, the conditional status is removed and the noncitizen spouse is recognized as a permanent resident. If the petition is denied the spouses may contest the denial of the petition in a removal hearing where the burden of proof will be on the government.[115]

149. The INA provides a hardship waiver to remove the conditional basis for spouses who are unable to comply with the joint petition and joint interview requirements if extreme hardship would result if the alien is removed; the qualifying marriage was entered into in good faith but the marriage has been terminated and the alien was not at fault in failing to file and appear jointly; or if the marriage was entered into in good faith and during the marriage the spouse or child was battered or was the subject of extreme cruelty by the citizen or permanent resident spouse.[116]

112. 8 U.S.C. §1186a.
113. *Ibid.*
114. 8 U.S.C. §1186a(c).
115. 8 U.S.C. §1186a(b).
116. 8 U.S.C. §1186a(c)(4).

150. Spouses of U.S. citizens are also exempted from the five-year period of permanent residence generally required prior to filing a naturalization petition. The spouse may file a petition for naturalization three years after being admitted as an immediate relative, and the two years of conditional status counts toward the period of time required for naturalization.

151. Marriages entered into while a noncitizen is in removal proceedings are presumptively invalid. Thus, a noncitizen generally may not receive immediate relative or preference status through a marriage entered into during removal proceedings until the noncitizen has resided outside the U.S. for a two-year period beginning after the date of the marriage.[117] The presumption may be rebutted by evidence that the marriage is valid and was not entered into to derive an immigration benefit by clear and convincing evidence.

II. First Preference: Unmarried Sons and Daughters of USCs

152. Unmarried sons and daughters of USCs are given the first preference in the family-sponsored immigrant categories. This category supplements the immediate relative category of children of USCs by adding children who are 21 and older as long as they have not married. All family-sponsored categories are subject to annual numerical limits and to per-country limits. The INA generally makes 23,400 visas available annually for unmarried sons and daughters of USCs.

153. The per-country limits provide that immigrants from a single country may not exceed 7% of the combined worldwide limits for family-sponsored and employment-based immigrants. Immigrants are "charged" to the country of birth, with some exceptions.

154. Annual numerical limits on the preferences and per-country limits are computed by USCIS through a complicated formula.

III. Second Preference: Spouses, Children and Unmarried Sons and Daughters of Permanent Resident Aliens

155. The spouse, children and unmarried sons and daughters of permanent residents constitute the second preference of family-sponsored admissions. A spouse and children (under 21 years of age) are a sub-group under this category, referred to as 2A's who are privileged in two ways: a certain number of visas are reserved for this category and 75% of the 2A's are exempted from the per-country limits. A spouse who falls under the second preference is subject to the same conditions and definitions as the spouse of a USC. Spouses of permanent residents, however, are

117. 8 U.S.C. §1154(g).

not eligible to file for naturalization in three years. The INA generally makes 114,200 visas available annually for second preference admissions. These categories are subject to per-country limits.

156. Unmarried sons and daughters of permanent residents constitute a subgroup referred to as 2B's. This category is not exempted from per-country limits.

IV. Third Preference: Married Sons and Married Daughters of Citizens and Their Spouses and Children

157. The third preference category consists of married sons and married daughters of USCs, who are allocated, as a general matter, 23,400 visas annually.

V. Fourth Preference: Brothers and Sisters of Citizens and Their Spouses and Children

158. The only other family relationship recognized as creating an immigration benefit under U.S. immigration law is for siblings of citizens, and their spouse and children. Brothers or sisters of USCs, if the citizens are at least 21 years of age, are allocated 65,000 visas annually.

§2. Administrative Procedures and Documents for Long-Term Residence

159. In order to apply for admission to the U.S., the petitioning family member (USC or LPR) or sponsor must complete the "Petition for alien relative" (Form I-130) and file it with USCIS. As of 2019, the filing fee for a Form I-130 is USD 575. Sponsors, USCs or LPRs, must be 18 years old (21 years for some relationships or preferences) and must have an income of 125% above the federal poverty level (in 2018, for a family of four the level was USD 31,375).

160. In addition, the sponsor must complete and file the Affidavit of Support (Form I-864), an enforceable agreement that guarantees that the sponsor will provide financial support to the beneficiary of the visa petition, to prevent the immigrant from becoming a public charge or requiring public benefits. When filed with the USCIS or DOS abroad, there is no filing fee for Form I-864; if the form is filed in the U.S. with DOS, DOS charges USD 120. Sponsors must provide supporting documentation with their support affidavit, including federal tax returns, evidence of income and employment.

161. If the beneficiary of the petition is already in the U.S. in another status, such as that of a nonimmigrant, the visa beneficiary must file for adjustment of status (Form I-485). An example of a nonimmigrant who may adjust status is a fiancé of a USC who is admitted on a K-1 visa (for fiancées) and marries the USC within ninety days of entry. Currently, the filing fee for a Form I-485 is USD 1,140. In addition, applicants are charged a USD 85 biometrics fee. Applicants must also undergo a medical examination at their own cost. In October 2020, the filing fee for the Form I-485 will be reduced to USD 1,130, but applicants will be responsible for an additional employment authorization fee of USD 550, and advanced parole for USD 590, all of which would have been secured prior to October 2020 under the USD 1,140 fee currently in place. The increase in fees scheduled to go into effect in October 2020 has been enjoined through litigation, and the Biden administration may abandon the fee increases.

162. The spouse and children of USCs or LPRs in an abusive relationship may self-petition for their own immediate relative or family-based preference admission through Form I-360. Form I-360 petitions must be submitted to the USCIS Vermont Service Center. If the petitioner is already in the U.S. and an immigrant visa is available immediately (in cases involving the spouse or children of USCs), the self-petitioner may file an adjustment of status application (Form I-485) concurrently with Form I-360. Self-petitioners are exempted from the filing fee. In order to qualify as a self-petitioning spouse, the spouse must be a person of "good moral character," must have entered the marriage in good faith, must have resided in the U.S. with the USC or LPR, and must have been battered or subject to extreme cruelty by the USC or LPR spouse. A self-petitioning child must establish that she or he is the child of a USC or LPR and that the parent is or was, during the two years immediately preceding the petition, a USC or LPR; that the child was subjected to abuse or extreme cruelty by the USC or LPR parent; that she or he is unmarried and under 21 years of age at the time the petition is filed; that she or he resided with the parent; and, if over 14 years of age, that she or he is of good moral character. Elderly parents of USCs may also self-petition if they have been battered or subjected to extreme cruelty by their USC son or daughter. The same general requirements of residence, proof of abuse and good moral character apply to elderly victims of abuse who wish to self-petition.

163. If the visa beneficiary is inadmissible but there is a waiver available for that ground of inadmissibility, then the beneficiary must file the application for waiver of grounds of inadmissibility (Form I-601) with supporting documents. The supporting documents will depend on the ground of inadmissibility. Most waivers currently require a fee of USD 930 but some waivers are exempted from the fee requirement.

164. All immigration forms are available on the web at www.uscis.gov. All forms contain thorough written instructions.

165. If the beneficiary of the petition is outside the U.S., the beneficiary must file an application for an immigrant visa and alien registration, DOS Form DS-260 with the consular office in the district in which they reside with supporting documentation. Each applicant must complete the DS-260 Form online after paying the visa fee.

166. Family-based visas are processed in accordance with their priority date (the date on which the petition for the visa was filed by the USC or LPR sponsor) and as visas for the corresponding preference and the beneficiary's country of origin become available. The per-country limits, thus, have a serious impact on visa applicants from high source countries like the Philippines and Mexico, which tend to have applicants in much higher numbers than are annually available. In addition, high source countries like the Philippines and Mexico also tend to exhaust the visa available on the basis of the family preference. The impact of both of these numerical caps affects the availability of visa for applicants from these countries. Backlogs may form in excess of ten or even twenty years. The backlog problem is complicated by delays in processing visa applications at the agency level. The DOS makes available on their website the Visa Bulletin, a monthly publication listing the priority dates for each country and any backlogs in visa preferences. Thus, persons immigrating to the U.S. from high source countries through the family preferences face long delays before they are reunited with the petitioning relative.

167. Congress responded to the visa backlog problem, to an extent, by making a new visa category available to certain noncitizens. The V visa, a nonimmigrant visa category that allows the spouse and children of LPRs who had filed for the visa before December 21, 2000, to enter the U.S. as nonimmigrants once their waiting times exceed three years. V-visa holders are granted authorization to work. V-visa status continues until the permanent resident visa becomes available.[118] If the permanent resident visa is ultimately denied, V-visa status terminates thirty days later. In addition, Congress provided for tolling of the time period in visa applications that are due to agency processing delays.

168. The visa backlogs create a problem for children who are beneficiaries of the family preferences but who risk, due to backlogs and visa processing delays, being too old to actually qualify for the visa as a child by the time the visa becomes available. "Child" under the INA means an unmarried child who is under the age of 21. Congress responded to this problem with regards to the children of USCs. For this category of family visa beneficiaries, their age is frozen as of the date the petition is filed, regardless of the child's age at the time the visa actually becomes available.[119] The age of children of LPRs that will count for visa purposes is their age at the time the visa becomes available; they will be allowed, however, to reduce their age by the amount of time the visa petition was pending due to processing delays at the agency level.[120]

§3. Legal Position of Long-Term Residents: Immigrants

169. Immigrants (LPRs), as a general matter, enjoy the same Constitutional and statutory protection enjoyed by USCs except the right to the franchise and the right

118. 8 U.S.C. §1101(a)(15)(V).
119. 8 U.S.C. §1151(f).
120. 8 U.S.C. §1153(h).

§4. Position of Family Members of Long-Term Residents: Immigrants

174. A spouse or child (unmarried and under 21 years of age) of an immigrant is admissible to the U.S. in the same status as the immigrant if accompanying or following to join the spouse or parent.[124] These family members will enjoy the same legal position as the immigrant once admitted. The only other family members to enjoy any benefit or preference under U.S. immigration law are family members who fit the relationships specified in the family preference categories: unmarried sons and daughters of LPRs. In order to facilitate migration of other family members, like married sons and daughters and siblings, the LPR will have to naturalize.

124. 8 U.S.C. §1153(d).

Part III. Right of Residence for Special Categories of Persons

Chapter 1. Nationals with Preferential Treatment

175. Nationals from countries that participate in the visa waiver program are given preferential treatment in nonimmigrant admissions. Over thirty-five countries are currently listed in the visa waiver program and they include the European countries, the Republic of Korea, and Australia.

176. Nationals of Mexico and Canada also enjoy preferential treatment under the U.S.-Mexico-Canada Agreement for business travelers. In addition, nationals of Canada do not need a visa to enter the U.S. Nationals of Mexico may obtain border-crossing cards that entitle them to enter the U.S. as is explained in paragraph 133 above.

Chapter 2. Students

177. Foreign students represent a substantial portion of nonimmigrant admissions to the U.S. Traditionally, the U.S. has valued and encouraged the presence of foreign students on its campuses. U.S. institutions of higher learning offer excellent educational programs as well as the opportunity to develop greater competence and fluency in English. The INA makes available three visa categories specifically for noncitizen students who wish to pursue studies in the U.S.: the F visa, the M visa and the J visa.[125] In addition, students enrolled in language or other courses of short duration (under eighteen hours per week) may also enter under the B-2 visa (visitor for pleasure). The F visa is intended primarily for academic students; the M visa is intended for vocational or other non-academic institutions; and the J visa is for exchange visitors.

178. F-1 visa is granted to students who have a place of residence in a foreign country which they have no intention of abandoning, who have qualified to pursue a full course of study and who seek to enter the U.S. temporarily and solely for the purpose of pursuing such a course of study at an established college, university seminary, conservatory, academic high school, elementary school, or other academic institution. The university or college determines a reasonable completion date for the particular program, and if the student is unable to complete the study program in that time, the student may request an extension from the university or educational institution. An extension will only be granted for compelling academic or medical reasons, such as changes of major or research topics, unexpected research problems, or documented illnesses. The university or educational institution the student attends is responsible for reporting extensions to USCIS.

179. Educational institutions that are approved by the U.S. government to participate in the F/J/M visa program are required to keep computerized data on students and exchange visitors as well as their accompanying spouse and children. Thus, in a sense, the educational institutions are responsible for maintaining data and records on student visa holders, rather than DHS. Students pay a fee to cover the costs of the program. The SEVIS is mandatory for any school wishing to admit a foreign student, and schools are required to notify DHS if there is any change in the status of the student.

180. Applicants for a student visa must demonstrate that they have been accepted by a school that has been approved by DHS in compliance with the SEVIS program; they must document that they have sufficient funds to support their educational pursuits; they must demonstrate that they have the preparation to pursue the full course of study for which they are being admitted; and they must have a sufficient knowledge of English or must have arranged to acquire training in English. The F-1 visa holder is permitted to work on-campus if the employment does not displace a U.S. resident. F-1 students are authorized to work in practical training that

125. 8 U.S.C. §1101(a)(15).

complements their degree program, like working as a teaching or research assistant. F-1 students may also seek off-campus employment through Optional Practical Training, which is temporary employment related to an F-1 student's major area of study for a period of up to twelve months. F-1 students are prohibited from taking up other employment off-campus except in cases of extreme financial hardship arising after arrival in the U.S.

181. The spouse and children of F-1 visa holders are eligible for an F-2 visa if accompanying or following to join the F-1 visa holder. Family members, however, are not authorized to work and may not attend school, except for children attending elementary or secondary schools.

182. Applicants for a student visa must obtain a SEVIS Form I20 issued in their name by an approved educational institution and pay the SEVIS Fee (I-901) to the consular office in their home state. Generally, the filing fee for the I-901 is USD 200 unless the applicant falls in a specified exception. Consular officers must verify the SEVIS Form I-20 (and verify that the student does not fall under any of the inadmissibility grounds) prior to issuing the F-1 visa.

183. The INA makes special provisions for Canadians or Mexican nationals, who maintain their place of residence in their respective countries, to attend educational institutions in the U.S. on a part-time or full-time basis by commuting daily to the U.S. This visa is made available for academic studies (F-3 visa) or vocational studies (M-3 visa). The spouse and children of border commuter students are not eligible for F-2 or M-2 status.

184. A smaller number of foreign students pursue vocational or non-academic courses of studies at vocational institutions in the U.S. under the M-1 visa. M-1 visa holders have a maximum of three years in which to complete their studies and are not allowed to accept employment, even on-campus, other than practical training. However, practical training may be obtained only after they have completed their course of study and may not exceed a period of six months. Their spouse and children may accompany or follow to join as M-2 visa holders. A spouse is not authorized to work or to undertake a full-time course of study. Children may attend elementary and secondary schools.

185. The J visa program is a cultural exchange program that includes the Fulbright program. The J-1 visa is designed to facilitate cultural exchanges between the U.S. and foreign scholars, professors, teachers, trainees, specialists, foreign medical graduates, international visitors and students. In addition, the J visa program accommodates au pairs and student work/travel programs. In order to be admitted on a J-1 visa, the nonimmigrant must participate in a program designated by the DOS's Bureau of Educational and Cultural Affairs. Admission is for the duration of the program. The spouse and children may accompany a J-1 visa holder with the J-2 visa. J visa applicants must have a foreign place of residence they have no intention of abandoning in order to qualify for the visa.

186. J visa holders may not adjust to another nonimmigrant or immigrant status before returning to their home abroad for two years if their participation in the cultural exchange program was financed wholly or in part by the U.S. or home government; the DOS designates their home country as requiring their services or skills; or they are coming to the U.S. to receive graduate medical training. J visa holders must also secure a SEVIS I-20 and the SEVIS fee (USD 180) to obtain J status. There is no filing fee for a J-2 visa.

187. The DHS recently proposed changes to the F, J and I visa holders that would cap the length of time visa holders may keep their status to four or two years, depending on a variety of factors, before having to petition to renew their status. Additionally, student visa holders from certain countries would be limited to a two-year period of authorized stay. This is a proposed rule that has not yet been formally adopted.

Chapter 3. Researchers

188. Both immigrant and nonimmigrant visas are made available for researchers. The immigrant visa categories available for researchers are described in Part VII of this monograph. In addition, researchers may be able to use the F-1 and J-1 visa, primarily, to pursue research opportunities in the U.S.

Chapter 4. Labor and Economic Migration

§1. Labor Employment

189. The immigrant visa categories available for labor employment are described in Part VII of this monograph.

§2. Seasonal Workers and Temporary Workers

190. The INA makes available a number of nonimmigrant visa for temporary workers. The primary provisions allow for temporary specialty occupation workers (professionals) (H-1B visa); temporary agricultural workers (H-2A visa); and temporary non-agricultural workers (H-2B visa). All temporary worker categories are subject to an annual numerical limit. Congress has been flexible, however, in increasing or decreasing the number of visa for temporary workers, particularly in the H-1B category. For the 2019 fiscal year, the numerical cap for regular H-1B is 65,000; and for H-2B it is 66,000.

191. The H-1B visa is available for a noncitizen worker whose stay in the U.S. is temporary to perform services (other than those described in (O) or (P) categories) in a specialty occupation.[126] A specialty occupation is defined in the statute as an occupation that requires theoretical and practical application of a body of highly specialized knowledge, and attainment of a bachelor's or higher degree in the specific specialty as a minimum for entry into the occupation in the U.S. Employers of H-1B's must file a labor certification application with the DOL attesting that it is paying the prevailing wage level in the area of employment or the actual wage level at the place of employment; that employment of the worker will not adversely affect the working conditions of similarly employed workers; that there is no strike or lockout; and that the employer has notified its employees of the filing. The statute provides that the DOL will issue the required certification unless it finds that the employer's attestation is incomplete or obviously inaccurate.[127] H-1B visa applicants file Form I-129 and pay a fee of USD 460, but the fee will rise to USD 555 in October 2020. H-1B visas have portability; that is the worker may change jobs after arrival in the U.S. H-1B workers may be admitted for up to six years. H-1B applicants may be admitted even if they have the intention to lawfully seek to become a permanent resident. The INA does not require that H-1B visa applicants have a foreign place of residence which they have no intention of abandoning.

192. The O visa category is available for workers with an extraordinary ability in the sciences, arts, education, business or athletics demonstrated by sustained national or international acclaim, and for motion picture and television productions, workers who have a demonstrated record of extraordinary achievement who seek to

126. 8 U.S.C. §1101(a)(15)(h)(i)(b).
127. 8 U.S.C. §1182(t).

enter the U.S. to continue work in the area of extraordinary ability. O visa applicants must complete an I-129 form and pay a filing fee of USD 460. O visa holders are admitted for a period of up to three years with possible one-year extension. The O visa category is not subject to a numerical cap.

193. The P visa category is available for artists, athletes and entertainers who seek to enter the U.S. temporarily to perform, teach or coach and their spouse and children. P visa applicants must complete an I-129 form and pay a filing fee of USD 460. The P visa category is not subject to a numerical cap.

194. Temporary agricultural workers may be admitted under the H-2A visa. H-2A visa holders must have a place of residence in a foreign country which the worker has no intention of abandoning. Employers must file for labor certification from the DOL: a certification that there are no U.S. workers willing and able to do the work and that the nonimmigrant's employment will not adversely affect the wages and working conditions of American workers.[128] Once DOL grants labor certification, USCIS must approve the employer's petition for H-2A workers before individual workers may obtain a visa for entry. H-2A workers must be provided with free housing, meals, return transportation and some type of workers' compensation insurance.[129] The H-2A and H-2B (described below) temporary worker programs are controversial; critics charge that they facilitate worker exploitation and provide little worker protection.

195. The H-2B temporary worker program is similar to the H-2A but applies to non-agricultural workers. The H-2B visa category includes landscaping workers, cleaners, housekeepers, construction workers and forestry workers. Employers seeking to employ H-2B workers must file for labor certification (for H visas). The work offered to H-2B workers must be temporary (a year or less), and the need must be seasonal, intermittent or a one-time occurrence. H-2B nonimmigrants are admitted for one year with one-year extension possible to a maximum of three years.

§3. Independent Economic Activities

196. The provisions on independent economic activities are described in Parts VII and VIII of this monograph.

§4. Investment Activities

197. The provisions on independent economic activities are described in Part VIII of this monograph.

128. 8 U.S.C. §1188(a).
129. 8 U.S.C. §1188(c)(4).

Chapter 5. Humanitarian Reasons

§1. Humanitarian Grounds

198. The INA allows the President to increase the number of refugees admitted in any one year if it is justified by humanitarian concerns or is otherwise in the national interest.[130] In addition, the INA grants the President authority to admit refugees in unforeseen emergency situations when it is justified by grave humanitarian concerns. Although the Trump administration sharply restricted refugee and asylum admissions, the Biden administration has signaled that it will increase refugee and asylum admissions.

§2. Unaccompanied Minor Children

199. Unaccompanied minors may enter the U.S. with a visa similar to adults. Minors seeking temporary visas to visit the U.S. are generally held to the same requirements and scrutiny as adults in the application process regardless of whether they are traveling alone or under supervision.

200. As part of the visa application process, an interview at the consular section is required for visa applicants from age 14 through 79. Persons aged 13 and younger, and aged 80 and older, generally do not require an interview, unless requested by the consulate. As explained in the various visa sections, minors must file the application for their respective visa themselves.

201. Federal statutes define an unaccompanied alien child as a child who has no lawful immigration status in the U.S.; has not attained 18 years of age; and has no parent or legal guardian in the U.S. or who is available to provide care and physical custody.[131] Unaccompanied noncitizen children who are detected attempting entry into the U.S. or are found in the U.S. without documents or authorization to enter will be detained by ICE and transferred to the Department of Health and Human Services Office of Refugee Resettlement within forty-eight or seventy-two hours. Children may be released to a parent, relative or responsible adult but if such placement is not available will continue to be detained until removed. Unaccompanied minor children may be placed in removal proceedings, but they may be eligible for asylum, withholding of removal, TPS, T visa (victims of human trafficking), U visa (victims of crime), and the Special Immigrant Juvenile visa (SIJ visa).

202. The SIJ visa was created by Congress in 1990 to allow eligible children to self-petition for admission. To be eligible for an SIJ visa the applicant must be unmarried and under 21 years of age, using the definition of child under the INA, rather than the statutory definition of "unaccompanied alien child." In addition, reunification with one or both parents must not be viable due to abuse, neglect,

---

130. 8 U.S.C. §1157(a).
131. 6 U.S.C. §279(g)(2).

abandonment or other similar bases. The applicant for an SIJ visa must be declared dependent by a juvenile court or committed to the custody of an agency or department of a state or an individual appointed by a state or juvenile court. The SIJ applicant must also demonstrate that it has been determined in an administrative or judicial proceeding that it would not be in the child's best interest to be returned to her or his country of nationality or last residence. SIJ applicants are excused from seven grounds of inadmissibility, including public charge, labor certification, entering without inspection, misrepresentation, stowaways, documentation requirements and unlawful presence; waivers of inadmissibility for other inadmissibility grounds remain available to them as well.

203. The U.S. and Mexico have an agreement that allows the U.S. to return unaccompanied Mexican children immediately without detaining them. In fiscal year 2009, CBP apprehended 101,952 juveniles, the majority along the US-Mexico border. Most of these children were from Mexico and were returned voluntarily without being detained. DHS detained 7,746. Most of those detained were male (74%) and between the ages of 15 and 18 (80%). In fiscal year 2014, CBP apprehended 68,541 unaccompanied non-citizen children along the southwest border. This represents a 77% increase from previous years. The majority of unaccompanied children apprehended came from Honduras, Guatemala and El Salvador, rather than Mexico. As in prior years, most of those detained were male and between the ages of 15 and 18. According to the CBP, that same year witnessed a 361% increase in family unit apprehensions, which numbered 68,541. Subsequently, the number of unaccompanied children apprehended has fluctuated. In 2018, CBP reported apprehending 50,036 unaccompanied minors and 107,213 family units. In 2019, however, CBP apprehended 76,020 unaccompanied minors and apprehended 473,682 family units, the latter a 342% increase from the prior year. 2020 numbers show a decrease in unaccompanied minor apprehensions, perhaps unsurprisingly in view of the pandemic: CBP reports only 30,557 unaccompanied minor apprehensions and 52,230 family unit apprehensions for 2020.

204. Approximately 21,400 unaccompanied minors came to the U.S. seeking refugee status in 2013. When an unaccompanied minor expresses a desire to seek asylum during immigration court proceedings, pursuant to the TVPRA of 2008, ICE will provide the minor written instructions regarding the filing of the asylum application (Form I-589) with USCIS. All asylum applications filed by unaccompanied noncitizen children will be adjudicated by USCIS, not immigration courts. Additionally, the TVPRA provides an opportunity for unaccompanied children, who did not previously file for asylum with USCIS and, who either have a pending claim or appeal, to have their asylum claim heard and adjudicated by a USCIS officer in a non-adversarial setting.

205. According to the Office of Refugee Resettlement Programs, they now house approximately 25,000 unaccompanied noncitizen children a year in their facilities, a significant increase from previous years. The average length of stay is approximately thirty-five days. In the fiscal year 2008, the number of children in their custody ranged from approximately 800 to 1,500. Of those, 78% were male and 225 were female. Thirteen percent were below the age of 14. The leading source countries in 2014 for unaccompanied noncitizen children were Guatemala (37%), Honduras (30%), and El Salvador (26%). Most are over the age of 14 and approximately 75% are boys.

206. The INA does not require immigration judges to appoint a legal representative to represent a minor in immigration proceedings. Often without pro bono services children must engage the immigration process on their own, regardless of age. Judges have wide discretion to create a courtroom atmosphere that is conducive to limiting a child's stress due to the adversarial setting. Child advocates have been critical of the U.S. practice concerning detention and removal of unaccompanied noncitizen children. This practice has been the subject of litigation and successful reform efforts. Detention centers, in particular, have been the subject of investigation and criticism.

207. No period of time in which a noncitizen is under 18 years of age is taken into account in determining the period of unlawful presence in the U.S. for the purpose of determining admissibility.

§3. Victims of Trafficking in Human Beings

208. Victims of human trafficking may be protected from removal through the T visa and the U visa. The T visa, created by the Victims of Trafficking and Violence Protection Act of 2000, is a special, nonimmigrant visa for victims of severe trafficking in persons, including sex trafficking, who are physically present in the U.S. as a result of such trafficking; who assist in the investigation or prosecution of those trafficking acts; and who would suffer extreme hardship involving unusual and severe harm if removed from the U.S. T visa holders enjoy nonimmigrant status for three years with possible extensions of time. After three years in that status in the U.S., they may apply for adjustment of status to permanent residence. The annual maximum number of T visas is 5,000. Human trafficking victims include victims of sex trafficking and labor trafficking. Immediate family members of trafficking victims are eligible for derivative nonimmigrant status. T visa holders are granted employment authorization.

209. The Victims of Trafficking and Violence Protection Act of 2000 also created the U visa for victims of criminal activity who have suffered substantial physical or mental abuse and who have assisted or may assist in the investigation or prosecution of the crime. U visa holders enjoy nonimmigrant status for four years, but they may apply for adjustment of status to permanent residence after three years of continuous presence in the U.S. in valid U status. The annual maximum number of U visas available is 10,000 for primary applicants. There is no cap for spouses, children and parents of children under the age of sixteen of U visa recipients, if they establish that receipt of a visa is necessary to avoid extreme hardship; or a government official certifies that investigation or prosecution would suffer without the assistance of the spouse, child, or parent of a nonimmigrant child. U visa holders are granted employment authorization.

Chapter 6. Asylum

210. The U.S. provisions on asylum generally are consistent with the 1951 UN Refugee Convention and the 1967 Protocol. As a general matter, the U.S. guarantees to persons granted asylum protection against refoulement, a French term used to denote the return of refugees to places where they are likely to be or have been persecuted, as well as the rights necessary to establishing or starting a new life in the U.S., like the right to seek employment and to be accompanied or followed by their spouse and/or children, and within a period of time, admission as a permanent resident, with the possibility of naturalization.

211. The INA provides that any noncitizen who is physically present in the U.S. or who arrives in the U.S., irrespective of such noncitizen's status, may apply for asylum.[132] The noncitizen must establish that she or he meets the definition of a refugee, as discussed below. While the application for asylum is pending, the noncitizen may not be authorized to work for the first 180 days from the time their petition for asylum is filed.

§1. Conditions for Admission

I. Refugee Status

212. An applicant for asylum has the burden of proof to establish that she or he is a refugee. The applicant must establish that race, religion, nationality, membership in a particular social group or political opinion was or will be at least one central reason for persecuting the applicant if returned to the country of nationality.[133] Noncitizens granted asylum are eligible to adjust status to permanent residence as long as they still qualify as a refugee and do not fall within the inadmissibility grounds.[134]

213. The INA defines "refugee" as any person who is outside the country of nationality or, if stateless, is outside any country in which such person last habitually resided, and who is unable or unwilling to return to that country because of persecution or a well-founded fear of persecution on account of race, religion, nationality, membership in a particular social group, or political opinion.[135] The statutory definition expressly bars any person who ordered, incited, assisted, or otherwise participated in the persecution of any person on account of race, religion, nationality, membership in a particular social group, or political opinion, from being considered a "refugee." The U.S. Supreme Court recently considered the question whether in interpreting the "persecutor bar" to those seeking asylum or withholding of removal, immigration courts could consider whether the noncitizen's assistance

132. 8 U.S.C. §1158.
133. *Ibid.*
134. 8 U.S.C. §1159.
135. 8 U.S.C. §1101(a)(42).

219. The grant of asylum is a discretionary administrative decision, as a general matter insulated from judicial review, except for claims based on statutory interpretation or constitutional rights. The statute provides that the testimony of the applicant may be sufficient to sustain the applicant's burden without corroboration, but only if the trier of fact finds that the testimony is credible and persuasive. Credibility is determined by considering the totality of the circumstances, and all relevant factors, on the demeanor, candor, or responsiveness of the applicant or witness, the inherent plausibility of the applicant's or witness's account, the consistency between written and oral statements, the internal consistency of the statements and with other evidence of record, including DOS reports on country conditions. On appeal, if the immigration judge does not make an explicit adverse credibility determination, the applicant has a rebuttable presumption of credibility.[141]

220. The Refugee Act does not specifically include sex or gender as one of the protected classifications. Nonetheless, gender-based claims have enjoyed some success under the "membership in a particular social group" category, including claims involving female genital cutting or mutilation and claims involving domestic violence. The definition also expressly includes "a person who has been forced to abort a pregnancy or to undergo involuntary sterilization, or who has been persecuted for failure or refusal to undergo such a procedure … ."[142] Under the Trump administration, the Attorney General issued decisions setting more stringent criteria for domestic violence-based asylum claims, and for claims involving gang-based violence affecting families. In addition, the DHS proposed new regulations that state that gender-based asylum claims are disfavored. This rule could extend to claims based on gender identity persecution or gender orientation persecution. The Biden administration is reconsidering these rules.

II. Subsidiary Protection Status

221. Subsidiary protection status is not provided other than through protection under the Convention Against Torture, or withholding of removal under U.S. law. In addition, persons may be paroled into the U.S. Persons granted withholding of removal or paroled into the U.S. have limited protection and do not enjoy the right to remain in the U.S.

III. Temporary Protection Status

222. The INA provides for TPS for nationals of countries in which there is an ongoing armed conflict if requiring their return to that country would pose a serious threat to their personal safety; or in which there has been an earthquake, flood or other environmental disaster resulting in a substantial but temporary disruption of living conditions; or in which the Attorney General (or DHS) finds that there are

141. 8 U.S.C. §1158(b)(B).
142. 8 U.S.C. §1101(a)(42).

extraordinary and temporary conditions in the foreign State that prevent the nationals of that country from returning in safety.[143] Noncitizens granted TPS are granted work authorization throughout the period they enjoy TPS. TPS has the effect of staying or halting removals. At least sixty days before the end of the period of the designation, the Attorney General (DHS) is required to review the conditions in the designated country to determine whether to extend the designation. To register for TPS applicants file an Application for TPS, Form I-821, and an Application for Employment Authorization, Form I-765. The fee for filing the form I-821 is USD 50. The filing fee for the Form I-765 for a worker is USD 410. The fee is scheduled to increase to USD 550 in October 2020.

223. In addition to being the national of a country designated for TPS, a noncitizen must have been continuously physically present in the U.S. since the date of the designation; be admissible or qualify for a waiver; have not been convicted of a felony or two or more misdemeanors in the U.S. In addition, the noncitizen must not have participated in the persecution of any person on account of race, religion, nationality, membership in a particular social group, or political opinion; must not have been convicted of a particularly serious crime; must not have committed a serious non-political crime outside the U.S.; must not pose a danger to the security of the U.S.; must not have engaged in terrorist activity and cannot have been firmly resettled in another country prior to arriving in the U.S. The noncitizen must register for TPS within the registration period set by DHS.

IV. Other: Relief under the Convention Against Torture

224. Relief under the Convention Against Torture supplements the relief available under the asylum and relief from removal provisions. Convention Against Torture relief applies to noncitizens who can show that it is more likely than not that she or he will be tortured if removed to a particular country. Under the Convention Against Torture, there is no requirement that the torture is related to persecution on account of one of the 1951 UN Refugee Convention protected classes (race, religion, nationality, membership in a particular social group, or political opinion).

§2. Procedures

225. Applicants for asylum and Convention Against Torture relief file Form I-589 either with the USCIS or with the immigration judge (EOIR), as explained above. If filed affirmatively, the determination as to whether to grant asylum will be made by the asylum officer, unless it is denied, in which case it will be referred to an immigration judge. If the application is filed in connection with a removal hearing, the immigration judge will adjudicate the application as part of the removal hearing. Immigration judge's decisions may be appealed to the BIA.

---

143. 8 U.S.C. §1254a.

§3. Legal Position

226. The legal position of noncitizens in the various categories differs according to their status, as explained above. Refugees or persons granted asylum enjoy work authorization and the right to bring immediate relatives with them; asylees may adjust to the status of an LPR one year after being granted asylum. Noncitizens with TPS enjoy benefits like work authorization and freedom from removal while they are in TPS, assuming they satisfy the applicable conditions. TPS, however, does not grant them any privileges in adjusting status to that of permanent residents. As soon as the government terminates the designation of TPS there is a risk of removal. Convention Against Torture relief effectively stays removal but does not necessarily entitle the noncitizen to any benefits under U.S. law, like authorization to work, bringing in immediate relatives, or even freedom from detention.

§4. Position of Family Members

227. Refugees and asylees may be accompanied by their immediate relatives. The legal position of their relatives will be the same as their own.

Chapter 7. Others: Diversity Immigrants

228. The INA provides 50,000 visas annually for permanent residence in the U.S. for diversity immigrants. Diversity immigrants are immigrants who come from countries with low rates of migration to the U.S. Countries that have high admission numbers to the U.S. are excluded from the diversity countries. Thus, diversity countries are countries that are designated through a complicated formula as countries that have not produced a significant number of immigrants to the U.S. The diversity visas are made available through a lottery. To compete in the lottery persons must have a high school education or its equivalent, or at least two years of experience in an occupation that requires at least two years of training or experience, within the five years preceding the application. Applications are completed online through the DOS' website. The applicants are selected on a random basis. Winners of a diversity visa may bring their immediate families. The diversity lottery is conducted annually.

229. For the 2016 diversity lottery program, the countries excluded were Bangladesh, Brazil, Canada, China (mainland-born), Colombia, the Dominican Republic, Ecuador, El Salvador, Haiti, India, Jamaica, Mexico, Nigeria, Pakistan, Peru, the Philippines, South Korea, the United Kingdom (excluding Northern Ireland) and its dependent territories and Vietnam.

Part IV. Loss of Right of Residence

230. The INA specifies the grounds that will cause a noncitizen to lose the right to continue residing in the U.S. in section 1227 of Title 8 of the U.S.C. Similar to the inadmissibility grounds, the statute states that noncitizens who fall within the specified classes are subject to removal. For the deportability grounds to apply (as opposed to the inadmissibility grounds), a noncitizen should have been admitted to the U.S. Whether a noncitizen is deportable or not will be determined through the removal process.

231. The U.S. Supreme Court treats deportation as a civil, not criminal, sanction. This means that the Constitutional protections that would apply to criminal proceedings generally do not apply in deportation or removal proceedings. The Constitutional protections that generally do not apply to deportation proceedings include the ex post facto clause and the 6th Amendment right to counsel. The ex post facto clause protects persons against retroactive application of the law, primarily criminal law. The 6th Amendment right to counsel guarantees persons accused and indicted of violating a state or federal criminal statute the right to be represented by counsel at the government's expense. However, to some extent, courts have recognized limited application of 4th Amendment rights in removal proceedings. The ex post facto and 6th Amendment guarantees, and all other Constitutional and statutory protection available to citizens in criminal proceedings, apply to the same extent to noncitizens in criminal proceedings. Since courts treat deportation as a civil proceeding, noncitizens are deprived of this protection in the removal or deportation proceeding. Although Congress may provide the same level of protection by statute, it has opted not to do so as a general matter. Congress has provided that noncitizens have a statutory right to counsel in removal hearings but not at the government's expense. To some extent, statutory protection may have been influenced by court rulings. The Supreme Court has held that the protection of the 5th Amendment due process clause in the U.S. Constitution applies to deportation hearings involving permanent residents, and the INA provides for a number of procedural safeguards in the removal process. The INA provides or allows for administrative appellate review as well as a minimal level of judicial review. Recently, scholars and litigants have challenged the practice of failing to provide counsel at government's expense to special groups facing removal, like children and incompetent adults, as failing to provide due process. Incompetent adults, currently, are entitled to a mental competency hearing before the immigration judge to determine whether they are in need of legal assistance in order to participate in their removal hearing. This is an unsettled area of law that is frequently litigated.

232. As will be explained more fully below, courts have treated detention as a necessary incident to the power to deport. The INA currently provides for mandatory detention of certain noncitizens facing deportation, and for discretionary detention of others. In recent years, the government has detained increasing numbers of noncitizens, even noncitizens who have not engaged in any criminal violations. These detentions pose tension for the U.S. system of law and there has been considerable litigation and commentary as to these detention trends.

233. As a general matter, if a noncitizen falls within one of the deportation grounds they are removable, unless an exception or waiver is available to them. Some grounds of deportation do not provide for waivers or exceptions. The statute provides a few avenues of relief from removal for noncitizens who are eligible to pursue them.

234. Criminal convictions result in a large number of removals. In *Padilla v. Kentucky,*[144] the U.S. Supreme Court held that an attorney's failure to advise a criminal defendant of the deportation consequences of a guilty plea may constitute ineffective assistance of counsel under the 6th Amendment. This case may make it easier for noncitizens who are rendered deportable on criminal conviction grounds to challenge the underlying criminal conviction, and, thus, to avoid removal. In *Chaidez v. United States,*[145] the Supreme Court held that *Padilla* did not apply retroactively to cases which are already final on direct review as of the date of the *Padilla* decision on March 31, 2010.

144. 559 U.S. 356 (2010).
145. 568 U.S. 342 (2013).

Chapter 1. Conditions under Which the Right of Residence Might Be Lost

235. The INA makes all inadmissibility categories applicable as grounds for deportability. Thus, under 8 U.S.C. §1227(a)(1) any noncitizen who was inadmissible at the time of entry or adjustment of status is deportable. The INA also targets any conduct related to immigration violations and renders such conduct a basis for deportation. Consequently, any noncitizen present in the U.S. in violation of the INA or any other federal law, or whose nonimmigrant visa has been revoked is deportable. In addition, any nonimmigrant who has failed to comply with the conditions of the status in which she or he was admitted or who has failed to maintain such status is deportable. Failure to comply with the conditions of admission in cases involving waivers to the public health inadmissibility grounds similarly render a noncitizen deportable. Any noncitizen whose conditional permanent resident status is terminated is deportable. Any noncitizen who has knowingly encouraged, induced, assisted, abetted or aided any other noncitizen to enter the U.S. without formal admission is deportable as well. The statute provides for a waiver from this deportability ground for an LPR who has assisted "only an individual who at the time of the offense was the alien's spouse, parent, son, or daughter (and no other individual) to enter the United States in violation of law."[146]

236. Procuring a visa through marriage fraud, if a marriage was entered into less than two years prior to admission and such marriage is annulled or terminated two years subsequent to the admission, renders the noncitizen deportable unless "the alien establishes to the satisfaction of the Attorney General that such marriage was not contracted for the purpose of evading any provisions of the immigration laws … ."[147] The statute provides a discretionary waiver for deportability on the grounds of inadmissibility at the time of admission through fraud or misrepresentation for immediate relatives of USCs or LPRs, as well as for VAWA self-petitioners.

237. The second major category for deportability grounds is criminal conduct. A vast array of state and federal criminal violations render a noncitizen deportable. Under 8 U.S.C. §1227(a)(2) a noncitizen is deportable if she is convicted of a crime involving moral turpitude within five years after the date of admission for which a sentence of one year or longer may be imposed. A noncitizen is deportable if convicted of two or more crimes involving moral turpitude, not arising out of a single scheme of criminal misconduct; if convicted of a violation relating to high-speed flight from an immigration checkpoint;[148] or if convicted for failing to register as a sex offender under 18 U.S.C. §2250. The statute authorizes a waiver for most of these criminal grounds, including convictions for aggravated felonies (more thoroughly discussed below), in cases where the noncitizen has been granted a full and unconditional pardon by the President of the U.S. or by the Governor of any of the states. The expansion of the criminal offense grounds of deportability has resulted

146. 8 U.S.C. §1227(a)(1)(E)(i), (iii).
147. 8 U.S.C. §1227(a)(1)(G).
148. 18 U.S.C. §758.

in substantial litigation, due to the government's aggressive use of these grounds to remove noncitizens. For example, the government has argued that driving while intoxicated is a crime involving moral turpitude, even if the state statute does not require a culpable mental state, but only negligent conduct. See, for example, *Hernandez-Martinez v. Ashcroft*,[149] holding that under Arizona law driving under the influence of alcohol is not a crime involving moral turpitude.

238. A noncitizen convicted of an aggravated felony at any time after admission is deportable. Aggravated felony is defined under the INA at 8 U.S.C. §1101(43) to encompass a wide variety of criminal behavior that may not qualify as an aggravated felony under either federal or state law. In some cases the definition encompasses conduct that may be treated as a misdemeanor under federal or state law. Aggravated felonies, for the purpose of immigration law, include traditional aggravated felonies like murder and rape, and other offenses that may or may not be treated as aggravated felonies in criminal law, like sexual abuse of a minor; illicit trafficking in a controlled substance, in firearms or explosive materials; a theft or burglary offense for which the term of imprisonment is at least one year; child pornography; gambling and organized crime offenses for which the term of imprisonment is at least one year; owning, controlling or managing a prostitution business; national security type offenses; offenses involving fraud or deceit in which the loss to the victim exceeds USD 10,000; tax evasion if the loss to the government exceeds USD 10,000; human smuggling (with a waiver to a first offense if the noncitizen committed the offense to assist only the noncitizen's immediate relative); offenses relating to fraudulent documents; offenses relating to failing to appear to serve a criminal sentence for offenses punishable by imprisonment for a term of five years or more; offenses relating to bribery, counterfeiting, forgery, or trafficking in vehicles for which the term of imprisonment is at least a year; offenses relating to obstruction of justice, perjury or subornation of perjury, including bribery of a witness, for which the term of imprisonment is at least a year; and attempts or conspiracy to commit any offense described in the section. The statute specifically provides that the definition of an aggravated felony "applies regardless of whether the conviction was entered before, on, or after the date of enactment of this paragraph." Thus, the statutory definition applies to conduct retroactively, so that even if at the time the conduct was committed it was not considered an aggravated felony, the noncitizen may be rendered deportable for that conduct if it is currently included in the definition.

239. The aggravated felony provisions have brought within their ambit numerous LPRs and other noncitizens. The provisions have immense impact on LPRs because a conviction for an aggravated felony bars most avenues of relief from removal. Although most criminal conduct will render an LPR deportable, certain LPRs may be eligible for cancellation of removal, explained further below. Cancellation of removal is barred to LPRs convicted of an aggravated felony. An aggravated felony conviction also renders noncitizens ineligible for asylum or voluntary departure, and their right to judicial review of their removal orders is limited. In

149. 329 F.3d 1117 (9th Cir. 2003).

addition, they are subject to a lifetime bar to reenter into the U.S., unless the Attorney General consents to their reentry. These provisions, thus, have been aggressively litigated by the government and noncitizens facing removal for relatively low-level criminal activity at the lower court level. In the first instance, immigration courts decide that a particular offense is an aggravated felony and then decide that the noncitizen is ineligible for cancellation of removal. The court denies the cancellation of removal petition and the noncitizen appeals on the grounds that the offense does not constitute an aggravated felony under the statute. A number of these statutory interpretation issues have reached the U.S. Supreme Court. Thus, for example, in *Lopez v. Gonzales*,[150] involving a conviction for a state law (South Dakota) offense of aiding and abetting another person's possession of cocaine where the offender was sentenced to five year's imprisonment under South Dakota law but was released for good conduct after serving fifteen months, the U.S. Supreme Court held that a state felony drug possession offense may not be treated as an aggravated felony for the purpose of the INA if the corresponding federal drug possession offense is a misdemeanor. In *Gonzales v. Duenas-Alvarez*,[151] the Supreme Court interpreted the aggravated felony theft offense to include state law "aiding and abetting" offenses, overruling a U.S. Court of Appeals for the Ninth Circuit ruling finding that California law distinguished between principals and aiders and abettors. In *Carachuri-Rosendo v. Holder*,[152] the Court held that a second simple possession of a controlled substance state law offense did not constitute an aggravated felony under immigration law because it did not qualify as a felony under the federal Controlled Substances Act; state prosecutors had failed to charge the prior simple conviction before trial and had failed to charge the second offense as a recidivist felony. The Supreme Court's holding that a particular offense is not an aggravated felony allows the LPR or noncitizen appealing the denial of cancellation of removal to be eligible for cancellation of removal and to pursue that form of relief. Cancellation of removal, however, is a discretionary decision vested by the INA in the Attorney General and exercised by the immigration courts. Many state offenses, moreover, have no federal corollary and there is a substantial lack of uniformity in how states treat criminal conduct, even as to whether conduct comes within the ambit of criminal sanctions. This non-uniformity creates challenges for noncitizens and for the counsel defending noncitizens in removal proceedings for criminal offenses.

240. The definition also includes a "catch-all" offense for "a crime of violence … [as defined in a federal criminal statute] for which the term of imprisonment" is at least one year. The federal criminal statute defines the term "crime of violence" to mean "an offense that has as an element the use, attempted use, or threatened use of physical force against the person or property of another, or any other offense that is a felony and that, by its nature, involves a substantial risk that physical force against the person or property of another may be used in the course of committing the offense."[153] Immigration authorities interpret this provision to

150. 549 U.S. 47 (2006).
151. 549 U.S. 183 (2007).
152. 560 U.S. 563 (2010).
153. 18 U.S.C. §16.

include conduct that is not commonly understood to constitute a crime of violence such as the state law offense of driving under the influence of alcohol. In *Leocal v. Ashcroft*,[154] the U.S. Supreme Court held that the state law offense at issue in the case did not constitute a crime of violence, using traditional canons of statutory interpretation, because the statute did not require intentional conduct. The Supreme Court's analysis indicated that the proper analysis for crime of violence purposes focuses on the statutory elements of the offense, what U.S. law describes as a "categorical approach," rather than the actual facts established at trial in the case. Which offenses constitute crimes of violence under the INA continues to be litigated. In 2018, the U.S. Supreme Court struck down the "crime of violence" provision that defined it "as any other offense that is a felony and that, by its nature involves a substantial risk that physical force against the person or property of another may be used in the course of committing the offense," referred to as the "residual clause," as unconstitutionally vague.[155] Thus, the permanent resident in the case, convicted of first-degree burglary under California law, was not deportable as an aggravated felon, and thus was eligible for cancellation of removal. The Supreme Court's ruling rested on a previous case in which the Court had struck down a similarly worded criminal statutory provision as unconstitutionally vague. The void-for-vagueness doctrine "guarantees that ordinary people have 'fair notice' of the conduct a statute proscribes," and protects "against arbitrary or discriminatory law enforcement by insisting that a statute provide standards to govern the actions" of the government actors.[156] The Supreme Court rejected the government's argument that because the case involved a removal proceeding, a less exacting standard should apply. The most exacting vagueness standard applied to removal, the Supreme Court reasoned, in view of the grave nature of deportation, which often amounts to lifelong "banishment or exile."

241. State misdemeanor offenses have been treated as aggravated felonies for immigration purposes by immigration courts and lower federal courts. In *Guerrero-Perez v. INS*,[157] the U.S. Court of Appeals for the Seventh Circuit upheld an immigration court decision holding an LPR removable as an aggravated felon for an offense under state (Illinois) law involving sexual conduct with a minor between the ages of 13 and 17 by a person less than 5 years older than the victim. As with most statutory rape offenses, the statute reached consensual conduct. It is not a defense to the offense that the victim consented. Under state law, the offense was a misdemeanor. The noncitizen had engaged in sexual conduct at the age of 19 with a 15-year-old girl. He was sentenced to thirty days work release and two years of sex offender probation. The immigration court treated the offense as one involving the aggravated felony of sexual abuse of a minor and child abuse and the federal court upheld that reasoning.

154. 543 U.S. 1 (2004).
155. *Sessions v. Dimaya*, 584 U.S. __, 138 S. Ct. 1204 (2018).
156. *Ibid.*
157. 242 F.3d 727 (7th Cir. 2001).

242. The criminal offense deportability grounds also make specific provisions for controlled substance offenses, in addition to those controlled substance offenses that may constitute aggravated felonies or crimes involving moral turpitude. The statute also provides that any noncitizen who, after admission, is convicted of a violation of (or conspiracy or attempt to violate) any state or federal law, or the law of any foreign country, relating to a controlled substance (as defined under the federal law for controlled substances at 21 U.S.C. §802) is deportable. The only exception to this catch-all drug-related provision is for "a single offense involving possession for one's own use of 30 grams or less of marijuana."[158] In addition, any noncitizen who is or, at any time after admission, has been a drug abuser or addict is deportable.

243. In addition, specific provisions render noncitizens convicted of certain firearm offenses, espionage, sabotage, or violations of the selective service system, among other violations, deportable. Specific provisions also render any noncitizen convicted of a crime of domestic violence, stalking, child abuse, child neglect, or child abandonment deportable. Noncitizens who violate protective orders in domestic violence cases issued by either civil or criminal courts are also deportable.[159]

244. The deportability grounds include particular provisions directed at document fraud, citizenship fraud and failure to comply with the registration provisions of the INA. The INA requires that noncitizens register with and notify USCIS of a change of address.[160] This is a continuing obligation that does not cease until the noncitizen naturalizes. Failure to do so risks a misdemeanor offense and 8 U.S.C. §1227(a)(3)(A) and (B) renders the failure to register and the failure to notify of a change of address grounds for deportation. In addition, document fraud in relation to immigration benefits renders a noncitizen deportable.[161] The statute makes available a discretionary waiver for the latter offense in cases involving a single offense, if the offense occurred solely to assist, aid, or support the noncitizen's spouse or child. The statute provides that a noncitizen who falsely represents himself to be a citizen of the U.S. for any purpose or benefit under any federal or state law is deportable. An exception is provided for a noncitizen whose parent(s) is/are USCs, who permanently resided in the U.S. prior to reaching the age of 16, and the noncitizen reasonably believed that she or he was a citizen of the U.S.

245. Another major category of deportability grounds revolves around national security grounds. Thus, any noncitizen who has engaged in any activity to violate any law of the U.S. relating to espionage, sabotage, or export from the U.S. of restricted goods, technology or sensitive information is deportable. Any noncitizen who has engaged in any other criminal activity that endangers public safety or

158. 8 U.S.C. §1227(a)(2)(B)(i).
159. 8 U.S.C. §1227(a)(2)(E).
160. 8 U.S.C. §1305.
161. 8 U.S.C. §1227(a)(3)(C).

national security or any activity in opposition to, or control or overthrow of the government of the U.S. by force, violence or other unlawful means is deportable.[162] In addition, participation in terrorist activities, as described in sections of the inadmissibility grounds dealing with terrorist activity, will render a noncitizen deportable, as will having participated in Nazi persecution, genocide or torture. The INA also vests discretion in the Secretary of State to deport a noncitizen whose presence or activities in the U.S. the Secretary of State has reasonable ground to believe would have potentially serious adverse foreign policy consequences for the U.S. The statute provides an exception similar to the exceptions provided in the parallel inadmissibility grounds.[163]

246. The deportability grounds also render any noncitizen who, within five years after the date of entry, has become a public charge from causes not affirmatively shown to have arisen since entry, deportable. In addition, any noncitizen who votes in a federal, state or local election in violation of federal, state or local law is deportable. An exception is provided to this ground for noncitizens who had a reasonable belief that they were citizens, whose natural parent(s) is/are USCs, if the noncitizen permanently resided in the U.S. prior to attaining the age of 16.

162. 8 U.S.C. §1227(a)(4)(A).
163. 8 U.S.C. §1227(a)(4).

Chapter 2. Legal and Administrative Procedures

247. For a number of noncitizens the INA provides an alternative to formal removal called voluntary departure.[164] Voluntary departure allows a noncitizen to voluntarily depart from the U.S. at the noncitizen's expense instead of being subjected to formal removal proceedings. Noncitizens who are removable under the aggravated felony or terrorist activity grounds are ineligible for voluntary departure. This avenue of relief is discretionary. Noncitizens may apply for voluntary departure at their own expense after removal proceedings have commenced. Voluntary departure decisions made before commencement of proceedings are made by DHS; if granted after proceedings have started, the immigration judge makes the decision. If granted voluntary departure, the noncitizen has 120 days in which to depart.[165] The advantage of voluntary departure to the noncitizen is that there is no formal removal order issued against them. A formal removal order results in a bar to admissibility of ten years unless the DHS agrees to allow them to reapply for admission. Moreover, reentry without inspection after one has been removed by order carries stiffer criminal penalties than simple entry without inspection, as is further explained below.

248. Voluntary departure is also available at the conclusion of removal proceedings for noncitizens who have been physically present in the U.S. for a period of at least one year immediately preceding the date the notice to appear was served; the noncitizen has been a person of good moral character for at least five years immediately preceding her or his application for voluntary departure; the noncitizen is not subject to removal as an aggravated felon or for engaging in terrorist activities; and the noncitizen has established by clear and convincing evidence that she or he has the means to depart the U.S. and intends to do so. Noncitizens permitted to depart voluntarily under this provision only have sixty days in which to do so. In addition, they are required to post a bond to be surrendered upon proof that the noncitizen has departed the U.S. within the sixty days period.

249. Noncitizens who fail to depart after being granted voluntary departure are subject to civil penalties of not less than USD 1,000 and not more than USD 5,000 and are ineligible for a period of ten years for voluntary departure, cancellation of removal and adjustment of status and registry.[166]

250. Noncitizens who are in the U.S. as LPRs, nonimmigrants, or without authorization and who are charged with being either inadmissible or deportable by ICE will be placed in removal proceedings.[167] Removal proceedings, the procedure used to determine whether a noncitizen may be admitted or, if admitted, removed from the U.S. are conducted by an immigration judge. The immigration judge has statutory authority to administer oaths, receive evidence and interrogate, examine and

164. 8 U.S.C. §1229c.
165. 8 U.S.C. §1229c(a)(2).
166. 8 U.S.C. §1229c(d).
167. 8 U.S.C. §1229a and §1229.

cross-examine the noncitizen and any witnesses. The immigration judge also has authority to issue subpoenas (orders requiring the appearance of a witness or evidence) and to impose civil money penalties for actions in contempt of the judge's proper exercise of authority.

251. Removal proceedings may take place in person with all parties physically present in an immigration courtroom; where all parties agree in the absence of the noncitizen; through video conference; or through telephone conference if the noncitizen consents after having been informed of his right to proceed in person or through video conference. Many removal cases involving detained noncitizens are done through video conference. The practice of holding removal hearings through video conferencing has been sharply criticized and has been challenged through litigation. During the COVID-19 pandemic, the rate of cases heard through telephonic or video conferencing has increased. The practice will continue to be the subject of litigation.

252. Noncitizens may be represented at no expense to the government by counsel of their choice authorized to practice in such proceedings. Many, if not most, noncitizens placed in removal proceedings cannot afford to pay for private counsel, and there are an insufficient number of attorneys in the U.S. willing and able to represent noncitizens in removal hearings. Thus, most noncitizens represent themselves in removal hearings. Given the complexities of U.S. immigration law, the complicated legal issues that come up because of the INA's reliance on state criminal law (which is likely to be different for each state) and federal criminal law in both the inadmissibility grounds and the deportability grounds, the fact that many noncitizens are not fluent in English and the fact that many noncitizens, as explained below, will be detained during their removal hearing creates a heavy burden for noncitizens and makes it unlikely that they will prevail in defending against a removal charge.

253. The INA does guarantee the noncitizen a reasonable opportunity to examine the evidence against her or him, to present evidence on her or his behalf, and to cross-examine the government's witnesses. The statute specifically exempts from the right to examine evidence, national security information. The statute requires that a complete record shall be kept of all testimony and evidence produced at the proceedings.[168]

254. The INA provides for an order of removal to issue if the noncitizen fails to appear at a removal hearing, as long as the government can establish by clear and convincing evidence that written notice to appear at the removal hearing has been provided to the noncitizen or her or his counsel of record. A removal order issued in such circumstances may be rescinded when certain conditions are met.

255. The immigration judge must decide whether the noncitizen is removable based only on the evidence produced at the hearing. The noncitizen has the burden

168. 8 U.S.C. §1229a(b)(4).

of establishing, if charged with inadmissibility, that she is "clearly and beyond doubt entitled to be admitted and is not inadmissible" under the INA; if charged under a deportation ground, that she is "lawfully present in the United States." The critical difference between a charge of inadmissibility and a charge under the deportation grounds is that in the case of the latter, the government (ICE) has the burden of establishing by clear and convincing evidence that the noncitizen is deportable. The statute provides that "no decision on deportability shall be valid unless it is based upon reasonable, substantial, and probative evidence."[169]

256. Removal proceedings are initiated with a notice to appear in immigration court, Form I-862. The notice must specify the nature of the proceedings against the noncitizen, the legal authority under which the proceedings are conducted; the acts or conduct alleged to be in violation of law; the charges against the noncitizen and the statutory provisions alleged to have been violated; that the noncitizen may be represented by counsel and that she or he will be provided with time to secure counsel; a list of counsel willing to serve free of charge; that the noncitizen must provide the government with a current address or telephone number; the consequences for failing to do so and for failing to appear; and the time and place at which the proceedings will be held.[170] This notice shall be given in person to the noncitizen (easily done if she or he is detained as many noncitizens in removal proceedings will be) or through service by mail to the noncitizen or to her or his counsel of record. The statute specifically prompts the government to initiate removal proceedings as expeditiously as possible after conviction in cases involving criminal offenses.

257. The INA authorizes the arrest and detention of a noncitizen during removal proceedings. The statute authorizes release on the posting of a bond or conditional parole for some noncitizens.[171] The statute also provides for mandatory detention during removal proceedings of noncitizens rendered inadmissible or deportable on criminal, national security or terrorism-related grounds, with some exceptions.[172]

169. 8 U.S.C. §1229a(c)(3).
170. 8 U.S.C. §1229.
171. 8 U.S.C. §1226.
172. 8 U.S.C. §1226(c); 8 U.S.C. §1226a.

Part V. Sanctions

258. Noncitizens indicted for criminal immigration violations, as with any other criminal violation, are entitled to all due process and other Constitutional protections accorded to criminal defendants in the U.S. criminal justice system, including a right to counsel at government expense. This monograph identifies immigration violations under the federal immigration statute. Other federal statutes sanction immigration-related criminal activity, but they are beyond the scope of this monograph. Increasingly, a number of states have enacted criminal statutes that sanction immigration-related activity. As a general matter, federal immigration law preempts state regulation of immigration, including criminal immigration statutes, unless authorized by federal law. State regulation of immigration-related activity is beyond the reach of this monograph.

Chapter 1. Sanctions

§1. Administrative Sanctions

259. The primary administrative sanction for attempting to irregularly enter the territory is to be detained and placed in removal proceedings. Alternatively, noncitizens may be granted voluntary departure. In some cases, the government may administratively close a case. The Trump administration issued a policy directive to immigration judges curtailing the use of administrative closures and proposed elimination of administrative closure. The Biden administration has proposed expansion of administrative closure.

260. Civil penalties may be imposed upon any noncitizen who is apprehended while entering (or attempting to enter) the U.S. at a time or place other than as designated by immigration officers of at least USD 50 and not more than USD 250 for each such entry (or attempted entry); in the case of a noncitizen who has already been subject to a civil penalty, of twice that amount.[173]

261. The primary administrative sanction for irregular stay or residence is removal. Alternatively, noncitizens who are present in the U.S. without documents or authorization may be granted voluntary departure, or, if eligible, may be granted relief from removal.

262. Noncitizens who are granted voluntary departure but fail to depart the U.S. within the time period specified are ineligible for voluntary departure, cancellation of removal, adjustment of status and registry.[174] In addition, they are subject to a civil penalty of not less than USD 1,000 and not more than USD 5,000.[175]

263. Noncitizens who reside in the U.S. without authorization or valid documentation may be rendered inadmissible for certain periods of time as described in the inadmissibility grounds dealing with immigration violations.

§2. Penal Sanctions

264. The first commission of an offense involving entry or attempted entry at an improper time or place is a misdemeanor offense under the immigration laws. Thus, noncitizens shall be fined or imprisoned not more than six months or both, for: entering or attempting to enter at a time or place other than as designated by immigration officers; eluding examination or inspection by immigration officers; or

173. 8 U.S.C. §1325(b).
174. 8 U.S.C. §1229c(d).
175. 8 U.S.C. §1229c(d).

attempting to enter or obtaining entry by a willfully false or misleading representation or the willful concealment of a material fact. Subsequent offenses, however, are felonies, providing for fines and/or a term of imprisonment of not more than two years.[176]

265. Noncitizens who have been denied admission, excluded, deported or removed, or have departed from the U.S. while an order of removal is outstanding and who reenter or attempt to reenter without express authorization from the U.S. authorities shall be fined and/or imprisoned for not more than two years.[177] Moreover, any noncitizen who reenters or attempts to reenter if her or his removal was based on a conviction for commission of three or more misdemeanors involving drugs, crimes against the person, or a felony shall be fined and/or imprisoned for not more than ten years.[178]

266. Noncitizens who have been removed on the basis of a conviction for the commission of an aggravated felony and who reenter the U.S. shall be fined and/or imprisoned for not more than twenty years.[179]

267. Noncitizens who have been excluded or removed from the U.S. based on national security grounds and who attempt entry or enter shall be fined and/or imprisoned for a period of ten years. This sentence may not run concurrently with any other sentence.[180]

268. Noncitizens, against whom a final order of removal is outstanding on the basis of the deportability grounds, (i)who willfully fail or refuse to depart within a period of ninety days from the date of the final order or removal under administrative processes, or if judicial review is had, then from the date of the final order of a court; (ii) who willfully fail or refuse to make a timely application in good faith for travel or other documents necessary to the noncitizen's departure; (iii) who connive or conspire, or take any other action, designed to prevent or hamper the noncitizens' departure; or (iv) who willfully fail or refuse to present himself or herself for removal shall be fined or imprisoned for not more than four years or both.[181]

269. In cases involving noncitizens who willfully fail to depart or who are deportable because of human smuggling, criminal offenses, failure to register, document fraud, or national security grounds shall be fined or imprisoned not more than ten years or both.[182]

270. The INA also creates a misdemeanor offense for willful failure to register, as required by immigration law, and for the failure to notify the government of

176. 8 U.S.C. §1325(a).
177. 8 U.S.C. §1326(a).
178. 8 U.S.C. §1326(b)(1).
179. 8 U.S.C. §1326(b)(2).
180. 8 U.S.C. §1326(b)(3).
181. 8 U.S.C. §1253.
182. *Ibid.*

changes of address.[183] Willful failure to register provides for a fine that does not exceed USD 1,000 upon conviction or imprisonment of not more than six months or both.[184] Failure to notify the government of a change of address results in a fine that does not exceed USD 200 or a term of imprisonment of not more than thirty days or both.[185]

§3. DETENTION

271. The INA authorizes immigration officers to order vessels or aircraft bringing noncitizens into the U.S. to detain the noncitizen on the vessel or at the airport of arrival and to deliver the noncitizen to an immigration officer for inspection.[186] Noncitizens may also be detained for physical and mental examination to determine whether the public health grounds of inadmissibility apply.[187]

272. Arriving noncitizens may, in the discretion of immigration officers, be permitted to withdraw their application for admission and depart immediately from the U.S.[188]

273. As a general matter, arriving noncitizens deemed inadmissible are denied admission and offered an opportunity to immediately depart voluntarily or are ordered removed unless the noncitizen indicates an intention to apply for asylum or a fear of persecution if she or he is returned to her or his country of origin.

274. Under the INA, a noncitizen may be arrested and detained pending a decision on whether she or he is subject to removal from the U.S.[189] ICE is responsible for arrest and detention of noncitizens pending removal. Noncitizens may be released on bond or granted conditional parole during their removal proceedings. Detention pending removal is essentially mandatory for noncitizens who are inadmissible or deportable on the grounds of criminal activity or national security/terrorism-related activity.[190] Detention pending removal is mandatory for noncitizens who apply for asylum, subject to the possibility of humanitarian relief. Recently, the U.S. Supreme Court reversed a federal circuit court ruling holding that noncitizens subject to mandatory detention have to be considered for bond after six months in detention. The Supreme Court rejected the appellate court's reasoning that due process concerns required detention authorities to conduct a bond hearing after six months of detention to determine whether the noncitizen is a risk to the community or unlikely to appear for future hearings. Instead, the Supreme Court construed the statute to require mandatory detention in the described categories and

183. 8 U.S.C. §1306.
184. 8 U.S.C. §1306(a).
185. 8 U.S.C. §1306(b).
186. 8 U.S.C. §1225(d).
187. 8 U.S.C. §1222.
188. 8 U.S.C. §1225(a)(4).
189. 8 U.S.C. §1226.
190. 8 U.S.C. §1226(c) and §1226a(a).

remanded back to the appellate court to consider whether lengthy mandatory detention pending removal hearings violated the Due Process Clause of the U.S. Constitution.[191]

275. Noncitizens ordered removed may similarly be detained until their removal is effected, unless granted permission to depart voluntarily.[192] If removal is impossible or takes longer than ninety days, the period of detention may be extended on a finding that the noncitizen is a risk to the community or unlikely to comply with the order of removal.[193]

276. Noncitizens who are charged with being removable may be detained pending their removal proceeding.[194] The statute provides that removal shall occur within ninety days from the latest of the following dates: (i) the date the order of removal becomes administratively final; (ii) if the removal order is appealed to a federal court and that court orders a stay of the removal order, the date of that court's final order; (iii) if the noncitizen is detained or confined (except under an immigrant process) the date the noncitizen is released from detention or confinement. Further detention is authorized beyond the ninety-day period if the noncitizen fails to procure travel documents or if there is a finding that the noncitizen poses a risk to the community or is unlikely to comply with the order of removal. Detention during the removal period is mandatory for noncitizens found removable pursuant to committing criminal offenses or on national security grounds.[195] Other noncitizens who are not removed within the removal period may be released subject to supervision.[196]

277. Noncitizens indicted with criminal sanctions will be subject to traditional criminal process and protection.

§4. Expulsion Measures

278. The primary expulsion measure is removal. Alternatively, noncitizens may be allowed to depart voluntarily.

279. The INA provides that once the government has ordered a noncitizen removed, the government shall remove the noncitizen from the U.S. within ninety days.[197] The removal period begins on the latest of the following dates: (i) the date the order of removal becomes administratively final; (ii) if a federal court issues a stay of the order in conjunction with an appeal of the order, the date of that court's final order; (iii) if the noncitizen is imprisoned (except under immigration process)

191. *Jennings v. Rodriguez*, 583 U.S. __, 138 S.Ct. 830 (2018).
192. 8 U.S.C. §1231.
193. 8 U.S.C. §1231(a)(6).
194. 8 U.S.C. §1231.
195. *Ibid.*
196. *Ibid.*
197. 8 U.S.C. §1231(a).

the date that the noncitizen is released from confinement. The removal period may be extended beyond ninety days if the noncitizen fails to obtain travel and other documents necessary for departure or through her or his acts prevents removal.

280. During the removal period, the INA provides for detention of the noncitizen. The INA provides for mandatory detention during the removal period for noncitizens found to be inadmissible or deportable under the criminal, national security or terrorist activity grounds.[198] If removal is not effected within the removal period, the INA provides that the noncitizen is subject to detention or supervised release beyond the ninety-day period.

281. If removal proceedings were initiated at the time of the noncitizen's arrival in the U.S., the noncitizen may be ordered removed to the country from which the noncitizen departed. Other noncitizens may designate the country to which they want to be removed. Alternatively, the noncitizen may be removed to a country of which the noncitizen is a citizen or national. The statute bars removal of a noncitizen to a country in which the noncitizen's life or freedom would be threatened because of her or his race, religion, nationality, membership in a particular social group, or political opinion.[199]

282. The INA provides for expedited removal of noncitizens who have been convicted of aggravated felonies, as defined under immigration law. The INA also provides for removal without a hearing of arriving noncitizens who are inadmissible for national security or terrorism-related grounds.[200]

283. Noncitizens applying for admission may be permitted to withdraw their application for admission and depart immediately from the U.S.[201] In addition, a noncitizen arriving in the U.S. and requesting asylum who is determined by an asylum officer to not have a credible fear of persecution shall be ordered removed from the U.S. The INA provides for mandatory detention of noncitizens pending the credible fear determination.

284. Voluntary departure allows a noncitizen to voluntarily depart from the U.S. at the noncitizen's expense instead of being subject to formal removal proceedings, subject to the discretion of DHS. Noncitizens who are removable under the aggravated felony or terrorist activity grounds are ineligible for voluntary departure.[202] Noncitizens in removal proceedings requesting voluntary departure before the conclusion of removal proceedings may also be granted voluntary departure by an immigration judge. If granted voluntary departure, the noncitizen has 120 days in which to depart. The advantage of voluntary departure to the noncitizen is that there is no formal removal order issued against them. A formal removal order results in

198. 8 U.S.C. §1231(a)(2).
199. 8 U.S.C. §1231(b)(3).
200. 8 U.S.C. §1225(c).
201. 8 U.S.C. §1225(a)(4).
202. 8 U.S.C. §1229c.

a bar to admissibility of ten years unless the DHS agrees to waive the ten-year bar. In addition, reentry without inspection after one has been ordered removed carries stiffer criminal penalties than simple entry without inspection.

285. Once a removal order has been entered, a noncitizen may still be granted voluntary departure. In order to qualify for this relief, the noncitizen must have been physically present in the U.S. for a period of at least one year immediately preceding the date that the notice to appear for removal was served; the noncitizen must have been a person of good moral character for at least five years immediately preceding the noncitizen's application for voluntary departure; the noncitizen must not be removable on aggravated felony or terrorist grounds; and the noncitizen must establish by clear and convincing evidence that she or he has the means to depart the U.S. and intends to do so. Noncitizens granted voluntary departure at the conclusion of a removal hearing have sixty days in which to depart from the U.S. Additionally, noncitizens must post a bond to be released on proof that she or he has departed within the sixty-day period.

286. Noncitizens who are in the U.S. as LPRs, nonimmigrants, or without authorization and who are charged with being either inadmissible or deportable by ICE will be placed in removal proceedings.[203] An immigration judge conducts removal proceedings. The immigration judge's decision may be appealed to the BIA. The BIA's decision may, with some limitations, be appealed to a Federal Circuit Court of Appeal.

287. Some noncitizens may be subject to expedited removal such as arriving nonimmigrants who are not granted voluntary departure, or who are not allowed to withdraw their application for admission, and who do not ask for asylum or evince a fear of persecution if returned to the country from which they came.

203. 8 U.S.C. §§1229a and 1229.

Chapter 2. Sanctions Against Persons Helping Illegal Immigrants or Residents

§1. Human Smuggling

288. Persons or entities who bring to the U.S. any noncitizen who does not have a valid passport and an unexpired visa may be administratively fined USD 3,000 for each noncitizen brought, in addition to the cost of transportation to return the noncitizen.[204]

289. Any person who knowingly brings to or attempts to bring to the U.S. any person to a place other than a designated port of entry; or who knowingly transports or moves or attempts to transport or who conceals, harbors, or shields from detection, or who encourages or induces, for commercial advantage or financial gain, a noncitizen who entered or remains in the U.S. in violation of law; or who engages in any conspiracy to commit any of the preceding acts shall be fined or imprisoned for not more than ten years or both.[205] In cases where the person in the commission of an offense causes serious bodily injury or places in jeopardy the life of any person, the term of imprisonment increases to not more than twenty years and/or a fine. In cases resulting in the death of any person, the sanction is death or imprisonment for any term of years or for life and/or a fine.[206]

290. In cases where the person transports, harbors, or encourages a noncitizen who entered or remains in the U.S. in violation of the law (but not for financial gain or commercial advantage), the sentence is reduced to imprisonment for not more than five years or a fine or both.[207]

291. Any person who, knowing or in reckless disregard of the fact that a noncitizen has not received prior official authorization to enter or reside in the U.S., brings or attempts to bring to the U.S. such noncitizen shall be fined or imprisoned for not more than one year or both.[208] If done for commercial advantage or financial gain, or if done with reason to believe that the noncitizen will commit an offense against the U.S. or a state punishable by imprisonment for more than one year, that person shall be fined or imprisoned for not less than three or more than ten years. For other violations, the sentence is at least five years, but no more than fifteen years. In the case of an offense in which the noncitizen is not immediately brought and presented to an appropriate immigration officer at a designated port of entry, the sentence is not more than ten years in the case of a first or second violation.[209]

---

204. 8 U.S.C. §1323.
205. 8 U.S.C. §1324(a).
206. 8 U.S.C. §1324(a).
207. *Ibid.*
208. *Ibid.*
209. *Ibid.*

292. In cases where the offense was part of an ongoing commercial organization or enterprise; where the noncitizens were transported in groups of ten or more; and the noncitizens were transported in a manner that endangered their lives or the noncitizens presented a life-threatening health risk to people in the U.S., those convicted of the offense may incur an additional sentence of up to ten years.[210]

293. Vessels, vehicles and aircraft used in the commission of the offenses described above, and the gross proceeds of the offenses, may be seized and be subject to forfeiture.[211]

294. Persons who knowingly aid or assist a noncitizen inadmissible as an aggravated felon under immigration law or on national security grounds shall be fined or imprisoned for not more than ten years or both.

§2. Human Trafficking

295. Importation into the U.S. of any noncitizen for the purpose of prostitution, or for any other immoral purpose, is prohibited. Any person directly or indirectly importing or attempting to import into the U.S. or holding or attempting to hold a noncitizen for any such purpose shall be fined or imprisoned for not more than ten years or both.[212]

296. The 13th Amendment to the U.S. Constitution prohibits slavery and involuntary servitude, except as a punishment for crime upon conviction, within the U.S. or any place subject to their jurisdiction.

297. Other federal criminal statutes prohibit human trafficking.[213]

---

210. *Ibid.*
211. 8 U.S.C. §1324.
212. 8 U.S.C. §1328.
213. 18 U.S.C. §§1592–1595; 18 U.S.C. §2421.

Part VI. Legal Remedies and Procedural Safeguards

Chapter 1. Legal Remedies in Case of Refusal of Right to Enter, Stay or Reside

298. Visa consular denials are generally not reviewable by a federal court. U.S. citizens petitioning for a visa for their noncitizen spouse residing outside the U.S. may be entitled to minimal process if a visa is denied. U.S. citizen spouses who petition for a visa for their noncitizen spouse have a protected liberty interest in living with the noncitizen spouse in the U.S. and are entitled to a facially legitimate and bona fide reason if the visa is denied.[214]

299. Arriving noncitizens may be allowed to withdraw their application for admission, subject to the discretion of immigration authorities, and depart immediately from the U.S.[215] In doing so they waive any right to a formal removal proceeding or expedited removal.[216]

300. Visa may be revoked after issuance and the INA does not provide for judicial review of such a revocation, except in the context of removal proceedings.[217]

301. Arriving noncitizens are subject to expedited removal.[218] Noncitizens subject to expedited removal are not entitled to a formal removal hearing before an immigration judge or to an appeal of the order to the BIA. An exception is provided for persons requesting asylum or evincing a credible fear of persecution if returned to their country of origin.[219]

302. Arriving noncitizens who are deemed inadmissible may be paroled under certain circumstances, if the immigration officer has reason to believe that the noncitizen may overcome the finding of inadmissibility.[220]

---

214. *Kerry v. Din*, 576 U.S. __, 135 S.Ct. 2128 (2015).
215. 8 U.S.C. §1225(a)(4).
216. 8 CFR §235.4 (2008).
217. 8 U.S.C. §1201(h) & (i).
218. 8 U.S.C. §1225(b).
219. 8 CFR §235.3 (2008).
220. 8 CFR §235.2 (2008).

303. Arriving noncitizens who are LPRs may be placed in formal removal proceedings, offered voluntary departure or, in the context of their removal hearings, be considered for relief from removal.

304. Immigration judge's decisions may be appealed to the BIA. The BIA may reverse or affirm an immigration judge's decision, summarily or by written decision. The BIA may also remand a case back to the immigration judge for further proceedings. The standard of review at the BIA level on matters of fact is for abuse of discretion. On matters of law, the standard of review is de novo. On matters of law, as a general matter, BIA decisions are subject to review in the federal circuit courts of appeals. As a general matter, federal circuit courts of appeal defer to the administrative courts on factual determinations.

305. If found removable from the U.S., certain noncitizens may be eligible for relief from removal. The primary mechanism for relief from removal is cancellation of removal. In addition, there are limited forms of relief, including voluntary departure, temporary stays and exercises of prosecutorial discretion. Exercises of prosecutorial discretion allow noncitizens to remain in the U.S. with work authorization but they do not vest lawful immigrant status on the noncitizen, who remains removable. Exercises of prosecutorial discretion include administratively closing a case, or electing not to initiate removal proceedings for certain cases. This form of relief is known as deferred action. Factors that may be considered in determining whether a particular noncitizen is a candidate for deferred action includes whether the noncitizen is an LPR, the length of time the noncitizen resided in the US, whether the noncitizen has a criminal history, humanitarian concerns, whether the noncitizen has past immigration violations, the likelihood of ultimate removal, and whether the noncitizen has served in the military. Temporary stays of removal are available pursuant to regulations (8 CFR (Code of Federal Regulations) §241.6). Noncitizens who move to reopen removal proceedings must move for a stay of removal as a stay is not automatic.

306. An order of removal is subject to limited judicial review. Noncitizens, as a general matter, subject to a number of exceptions, may appeal a final order of removal to a federal circuit Court of Appeals.[221] Generally, the INA prohibits judicial review of discretionary relief like cancellation of removal and limits judicial review over certain removal decisions, like those based on criminal offenses or those involving arriving noncitizens who are immediately removed.[222] The bar on judicial review applies only to discretionary decisions that are rendered discretionary by statute, not through regulations promulgated by agency action. Thus, in *Kucana v. Holder*,[223] the Supreme Court held that an administrative court's refusal to reopen a removal proceeding was reviewable by a federal court.

221. 8 U.S.C. §1252(a).
222. *Ibid.*
223. 558 U.S. 233 (2010).

307. A petition for review must be filed thirty days after the final removal order.[224] It must be filed with the federal Court of Appeals for the judicial circuit in which the immigration judge completed the proceedings. The federal Court of Appeals is authorized to stay the removal order pending the appeal.[225]

308. The restrictions on judicial review raise a number of Constitutional issues some of which have been litigated before the U.S. Supreme Court. Generally, the Supreme Court has interpreted restrictive statutes to allow judicial review of Constitutional and federal statutory interpretation issues. To some extent, then, like many INA provisions, the judicial review provisions continue to be the subject of litigation.

309. The INA provides that federal courts of appeals decide the removal petition on the basis of the administrative record. Moreover, the statute renders the administrative findings of fact to be conclusive "unless any reasonable adjudicator would be compelled to conclude to the contrary."[226] With regards to a decision concerning admissibility, the statute provides that it is conclusive "unless manifestly contrary to the law and an abuse of discretion."[227] Even removal orders based on a denial of asylum, discretionary decisions, "shall be conclusive unless manifestly contrary to the law and an abuse of discretion."[228]

310. Noncitizens who are removable may be eligible for cancellation of removal. A noncitizen applying for relief or protection from removal has the burden of proof to establish that the noncitizen satisfies the applicable eligibility requirements and that the noncitizen merits a favorable exercise of discretion.[229] The application for relief should be supported by credible and persuasive evidence, including the applicant's testimony.

311. The Attorney General may cancel removal in the case of an inadmissible or deportable noncitizen if the noncitizen has been an LPR for no less than five years; if the noncitizen has resided in the U.S. continuously for seven years after having been admitted in any status; and if the noncitizen has not been convicted of an aggravated felony (as defined in the INA).[230]

312. The Attorney General may cancel removal of, and adjust to the status of an LPR, a noncitizen who is inadmissible or deportable from the U.S. if the noncitizen has been physically present in the U.S. for a continuous period of not less than ten years immediately preceding the date of the application; has been a person of good moral character during that period; has not been convicted of an offense under the

224. 8 U.S.C. §1252(b).
225. *Ibid.*
226. 8 U.S.C. §1252(b)(4)(B).
227. 8 U.S.C. §1252(b)(4)(C).
228. 8 U.S.C. §1252(b)(4)(D).
229. 8 U.S.C. §1229a(c)(4).
230. 8 U.S.C. §1229b(a).

criminal offense or failure to register and document fraud admissibility or deportability grounds; and who establishes that removal would result in exceptional and extremely unusual hardship to the noncitizen's spouse, parent, or child, who is a USC or LPR.[231]

313. The Attorney General may cancel removal of, and adjust to the status of an LPR, a noncitizen who is inadmissible or deportable from the U.S. if the noncitizen demonstrates that the noncitizen has been battered or subjected to extreme cruelty by a USC or LPR spouse or parent; if the noncitizen has been battered or subjected to extreme cruelty by a USC or LPR whom the noncitizen intended to marry, but whose marriage is not legitimate because of the USC or LPR's bigamy; if the noncitizen has been physically present in the U.S. for a continuous period of not less than three years immediately preceding the date of the application; the noncitizen has been a person of good moral character during such period; the noncitizen is not inadmissible or deportable on criminal offense and national security grounds, or deportable for failing to register or document fraud grounds, and has not been convicted of an aggravated felony.[232]

314. In addition to cancellation of removal, persons who are inadmissible or deportable may be granted voluntary departure, temporary stay, or deferred action.

315. In 2012, DHS announced the Deferred Action for Childhood Arrivals (DACA), a form of deferred action designed to defer removal of noncitizens out of lawful status under the age of 31 as of June 15, 2012, who have entered the U.S. without inspection before the age of 16 (and before June 15, 2012). DACA required that the noncitizens have continuously resided in the U.S. since June 15, 2007; were physically present in the U.S. on June 15, 2012; were currently in school, or a high school graduate, or a graduate equivalency degree or general educational development test, or an honorably discharged veteran. In addition, in order to qualify for DACA, applicants could not have a felony or significant misdemeanor conviction and could not pose a threat to public safety or national security. DACA was implemented on August 15, 2012. Between August 2012 and September 2013, USCIS approved 514,800 DACA requests out of a total 580,000 accepted. The majority of DACA applicants came from Mexico and a substantial number of applicants (277,000) were 19 years and under. California had the largest number of requests accepted for DACA relief. DACA relief continues to be available.

316. In November 2014, President Barak Obama announced an expansion of DACA that would allow adults over the age of 31 to take advantage of the DACA program. In addition, President Barak Obama granted deferred action for parents of U.S. citizens and lawful permanent residents: Deferred Action for Parents of Americans and Lawful Permanent Residents (DAPA). DAPA was halted as a result of litigation, which resulted in a federal appellate court judgment that declared the

231. 8 U.S.C. §1229b(b)(1).
232. 8 U.S.C. §1229b(b)(2).

expansion invalid. On appeal to the U.S. Supreme Court, the Court was equally divided, so no majority was reached and the lower court ruling was affirmed.

317. In September 2017, the Trump administration rescinded the DACA program. Persons who had been granted DACA status continue to enjoy it and have been allowed to renew that status, pending litigation. Litigants challenged the cessation of DACA and a federal district court issued a preliminary injunction in January 2018, upheld by the Ninth Circuit Court of Appeals in November 2018. The Ninth Circuit Court reasoned that the administration's cessation of the program was based on an incorrect view of the law.[233] On appeal, the U.S. Supreme Court ruled that the DHS's rescission of the DACA program was arbitrary and capricious, and thus invalid.[234] Subsequently, the DHS announced that it is reconsidering whether to rescind DACA again, but rejecting all initial requests for DACA relief. DHS is continuing to renew existing applications but only for one year.

233. *Regents of the Univ. of Cal. v. USDHS*, No. 18-15068 (9th Cir. Nov. 8, 2018).
234. *Department of Homeland Security et al. v. Regents of the Univ. of Cal. et al.*, 591 U.S. __ (2020).

Chapter 2. Procedural Safeguards

318. In the administrative removal process, noncitizens are guaranteed certain statutory rights, including the right to notice and a hearing; the right to be represented by counsel at the noncitizen's expense; the right to be informed of the nature of the charges; a reasonable opportunity to examine the government's evidence; and the right to present evidence and to cross-examine government witnesses. However, the statute specifically authorizes the use of secret national security evidence in removal proceedings, and courts, generally, have upheld the use of such secret evidence.[235] The noncitizen is also entitled to a complete record of all testimony and evidence produced at the proceedings.

319. In cases involving removals on the basis of the inadmissibility grounds, the burden is on the noncitizen to establish that the noncitizen is clearly and beyond doubt entitled to be admitted and that she or he is not inadmissible; or by clear and convincing evidence, that the noncitizen is lawfully present in the U.S. pursuant to a prior admission.[236]

320. In cases involving removals on the basis of the deportability grounds, the burden is on the government to establish by clear and convincing evidence that the LPR is deportable. "No decision on deportability shall be valid unless it is based upon reasonable, substantial, and probative evidence."[237]

321. The immigration judge is required to inform the noncitizen of all the rights and protection guaranteed under the INA. If the immigration judge decides that the noncitizen is to be removed, the judge must inform the noncitizen of his right to appeal that decision to the BIA and of the consequences for failure to depart under the order of removal, including civil and criminal penalties.[238]

322. The noncitizen is permitted to file one motion to reconsider an immigration judge's decision that the noncitizen is removable from the U.S. The motion must be filed within thirty days of the date of a final administrative order of removal.[239] In addition, a noncitizen may file one motion to reopen proceedings. Motions to reopen generally are granted when new facts, not available at the time of the original hearing, become available and the noncitizen seeks to introduce the new evidence. Motions to reopen may be filed within ninety days of the date of entry of a final administrative order of removal. However, there is no time limit on the filing of a motion to reopen if it is based on changed country conditions arising in the country of nationality or the country to which removal has been ordered and a claim for asylum.[240] Deadlines are statutorily waived for noncitizen spouses, children or parents

235. 8 U.S.C. §1229a(b)(4).
236. 8 U.S.C. §1229a(c)(2).
237. 8 U.S.C. §1229a(c)(3).
238. 8 U.S.C. §1229a(c)(5).
239. 8 U.S.C. §1229a(c)(6).
240. 8 U.S.C. §1229a(c)(7).

who have been subjected to battering by the USC or LPR spouse or parent. In *Kucana v. Holder*,[241] the Supreme Court held that the BIA's denial of a motion to reopen removal is subject to judicial review.

323. The U.S. Supreme Court held that noncitizens who are in the U.S. and who have been admitted to the U.S. are entitled to protection under the 5th Amendment due process clause of the U.S. Constitution. In addition, in the context of criminal process, whether in federal or state systems, noncitizens are entitled to the same procedural protection as USCs. Noncitizens in federal criminal process, however, may have removal imposed as a sanction for their criminal conviction by the federal judge as part of sentencing.[242]

241. 558 U.S. 233 (2010).
242. 8 U.S.C. §1228(c).

Part VII. Access to the Labor Market

Chapter 1. Overview of Applicable Legislation

324. As a general matter, noncitizens admitted as LPRs are authorized to work in the U.S. for any employer as long as they maintain their status as an LPR. Thus, noncitizens admitted as LPRs either under the family-based preferences or the employment-based preferences further explained below are given general authorization to work in the U.S. as one of the conditions or terms of their admission for permanent residence.[243] Although the authorization to work is implicit in their admission, most noncitizen immigrant admissions are required to apply for an employment authorization document Form I-765 to USCIS. Even noncitizens admitted under most of the employment-based preference categories are not required to stay in the employment relationship that was relied on to admit them to the U.S. as LPRs. Once they are admitted they may pursue whatever employment opportunities are available to them.

325. Noncitizens who are admitted as nonimmigrants in the temporary employment categories are also authorized to work, but their authorization will be limited by the terms of the particular nonimmigrant category.[244] These nonimmigrant workers will be authorized to work for the specific employer who petitioned for their admission and the authorization is temporary.

326. Other noncitizens who are admitted or paroled into the U.S. must apply to USCIS for employment authorization through Form I-765 and pay a filing fee of USD 410 (plus a biometric services fee of USD 85 for a total of USD 495), depending on the age of the applicant.[245]

327. The INA provides employment-based immigrant preferences that make it possible for noncitizens to be admitted as permanent residents on the basis of their professional or employment characteristics, or on the basis of an actual employment relationship with a U.S. employer. The process for admission to permanent residency through employment visas differs from that of family-based preferences, and the number of visas allotted for the employment categories is less than for family-based categories. Once admitted as a permanent resident, the noncitizen

243. 8 CFR §274a.12(a).
244. 8 CFR §274a.12(b).
245. 8 CFR §274a.12(c).

enjoys all benefits of permanent residence, in particular, becoming eligible for naturalization at the end of five years of permanent residence.

328. No federal statute prohibits noncitizens in the U.S. from working, and it is not a criminal act for a noncitizen to work in the U.S. without authorization. But IRCA prohibits all U.S.-based employers from employing any person who is not authorized to work in the U.S.[246] IRCA also imposes stringent verification of authorization and record-keeping requirements on U.S. employers.[247] Increasingly, states have sought to restrict employment of undocumented noncitizens by imposing state criminal penalties on noncitizens who work without work authorization. Recently, the Supreme Court struck down a state statute that criminally prohibited noncitizens from working without work authorization on the grounds that this kind of statute is preempted by IRCA because it is inconsistent with IRCA's treatment of unauthorized workers.[248]

329. In anticipation of increased discrimination against workers on the basis of national origin, IRCA enacted anti-discrimination provisions, which supplement other federal anti-discrimination statutes.[249]

330. Other employment-related federal statutes protect noncitizen workers, even unauthorized workers, from worker abuse. The statutes that protect noncitizen workers include Title VII of the Civil Rights Act of 1964,[250] which prohibits employers of at least fifteen employees from discriminating on the basis of sex, race, color, national origin and religion; the Fair Labor Standards Act,[251] which imposes minimum wage and hours requirements on employers; the Occupational Safety and Health Act,[252] which regulates the safety of employees and workplaces in the U.S.; the Social Security Act,[253] which provides health and retirement benefits to workers; the Americans with Disabilities Act;[254] and workmen's compensation state systems, which provide compensation to employees who are injured on the job. Workers may also pursue whatever state law legal causes of action are available to them, like a cause of action for wrongful termination or infliction of emotional distress. The extent to which nonimmigrant, unauthorized or undocumented workers may be eligible for remedies or benefits under these statutes may not be settled and is beyond the scope of this monograph. As a general matter, unauthorized or undocumented noncitizens are not entitled to benefits under federal law. Generally, they are entitled to protection from abusive, unsafe or exploitative practices.

246. 8 U.S.C. §1324a.
247. 8 U.S.C. §1324a(b).
248. *Arizona v. United States*, 567 U.S. 387 (2012).
249. 8 U.S.C. §1324b.
250. 42 U.S.C. §§2000 et seq.
251. 29 U.S.C. §§201–219.
252. 29 U.S.C. §§651–678.
253. 42 U.S.C. §§301, 401, 1301 et seq.
254. 42 U.S.C. §§12101–12213.

Chapter 2. Conditions for Entitlement to Work in the Country as an Employed Person

§1. General Conditions

331. The general conditions for immigrant workers, noncitizens who are admitted for permanent residence on the basis of an employment relationship are specified in the INA. The first preference category is for "priority workers."[255] Priority workers include noncitizens with an extraordinary ability in the sciences, arts, education, business or athletics; outstanding professors and researchers; and multinational executives and managers.

332. In order to be considered a noncitizen with an extraordinary ability in the sciences, arts, education, business or athletics, the noncitizen must demonstrate sustained national or international acclaim and that her or his achievements have been recognized in the field through extensive documentation. The noncitizen must intend to continue work in the U.S. in the area of extraordinary ability and the statute requires that the noncitizen's entry into the U.S. will substantially benefit prospectively the U.S.

333. For a noncitizen to qualify as an outstanding professor and researcher, she or he must be recognized internationally as outstanding in a specific academic area; must have at least three years of experience in teaching or research in the academic area; and must seek to enter the U.S. for a tenured or tenure track position at a university to teach or conduct research in the academic area or for a comparable position to conduct research.

334. For a noncitizen to qualify as a multinational executive and manager, she or he must, in the three years preceding the time of the application for admission into the U.S., have been employed for at least one year by a firm or corporation, and she or he must be seeking to enter the U.S. in order to continue to render services to the same employer in a capacity that is managerial or executive.

335. First preference employment petitioners may self-petition for an immigrant visa. They do not need an offer of employment at the time they petition in order to qualify for the immigrant visa.

336. The second preference category is for members of the professions holding advanced degrees or noncitizens of exceptional ability. Second preference applicants generally must have a job offer from a U.S. employer and must obtain labor certification, a finding from the DOL that able, willing, and qualified American workers are not able and willing to fill the position and that the applicant's employment will not adversely affect the wages and working conditions of comparable U.S.

255. 8 U.S.C. §1153(b)(1).

workers. The statute provides a waiver from the requirement that second preference applicants have a job offer and labor certification, when it is deemed to be in the national interest.

337. The third preference consists of skilled workers, professionals and other workers. Visas for other workers (generally unskilled or low-skilled workers) are capped at 10,000. Skilled workers perform work that generally requires at least two years of training or experience, not work of a temporary or seasonal nature, for which qualified workers are not available in the U.S. Professionals are those individuals who hold baccalaureate degrees and who are members of the professions. Other workers are those workers who perform unskilled labor, not of a temporary or seasonal nature, for which qualified workers are not available in the U.S. Skilled workers, professionals and other workers must have a job offer and must obtain labor certification from the DOL, a finding that there are no able and willing U.S. workers for the position and that the applicant's employment will not adversely affect the wages and working conditions of comparable U.S. workers.

338. All of the above preferences receive 28.6% of all the employment-based visas, generally 40,000 visas annually for each preference, and any unused visa from other specified preferences, with the exception of "other workers" who are only allocated 10,000 visas annually.

339. The fourth employment preference is for special immigrants, certain religious workers and certain long-term foreign employees of the U.S. government. This category is allocated 7.1% of the employment-based visas. Religious workers include noncitizens who will work as ministers; noncitizens who will work for a religious organization in a professional capacity, in a religious vocation or occupation; and noncitizens who will work for a bona fide religious organization in a religious vocation or occupation.

340. The fifth preference is reserved for employment creation. This preference category requires that the noncitizen seeks to enter the U.S. for the purpose of engaging in a new commercial enterprise in which the noncitizen has invested at least USD 1 million and which will benefit the U.S. economy and create full-time employment for not fewer than ten USCs or LPRs within two years. This preference category is allotted 7.1% of the employment-based visas, generally 10,000 visas. This category, however, has not exhausted its annual allocation of visas and, in fact, has generated very little migration to the U.S. until recently. In 2013, for example, fifth preference employment creation admissions were 243; in 2014, the number decreased to 161. In 2015, however, 10,188 noncitizens were admitted to permanent residence under the fifth preference. In 2016, 9,863 permanent residents were admitted in this category and 9,877 were admitted in 2017. In 2018, 9,623 persons were admitted to permanent residence under the fifth preference.

§2. Administrative Rules and Procedures

341. The first preference employment admission categories may self-petition and may have their visa application determined without certification from the DOL. Most of the other employment-based admission categories must have an offer of employment and the employer must file a petition with USCIS and for labor certification or attestation with the DOL.

342. Employers seeking admission for a noncitizen in the employment-based preferences, or in the case of noncitizens who may self-petition priority workers, must file a Form I-140 with USCIS and pay a filing fee of USD 580. For employment immigrant visa that requires labor certification, the employer must submit labor certification from the DOL with Form I-140, in addition to the supporting documentation necessary to satisfy the terms of the particular preference category. Noncitizens who seek adjustment of status may file a Form I-485 (adjustment of status) concurrently with Form I-140 if the immigrant visa is immediately available. The employment-based immigrant visa categories tend to be current; that is, they do not often experience the severe backlogs that plague the family-based immigrant visa. Thus, for some noncitizens, it may make sense to file both forms concurrently.

343. Noncitizens petitioning for admission as a special immigrant religious worker under the fourth employment-based preference must file Form I-360, Petition for Classification as a Special Immigrant with USCIS, and pay a filing fee of USD 405, unless they meet an exception. The petition should be accompanied by evidence establishing that the terms of the visa are met. Noncitizens who are petitioning as former employees of the U.S. government under the fourth employment-based preference must file their petitions with the Secretary of the DOS.

344. Noncitizens petitioning for admission under the fifth employment-based preference for immigrant investors must file a petition with USCIS using Form I-526 and pay a filing fee of USD 1,500. The petition must be submitted with evidence that the commercial enterprise has been established; that the petitioner has invested in the enterprise; that the capital used to invest was acquired lawfully; that the commercial enterprise has created, or will create, at least ten full-time positions for qualified employees; that the petitioner is an active investor and that she or he will be involved in the management of the enterprise; if the enterprise is in a targeted area, proof that the area satisfies the requirements of a targeted area, and any other evidence deemed necessary to process the application.[256]

345. Noncitizens admitted as immigrant investors, and their spouses and children are admitted conditionally for two years and must petition for removal of conditional status within ninety days immediately preceding the second anniversary of the noncitizen's having been granted such status.[257] Failure to apply for removal of the conditional status will result in automatic termination of lawful status in the

256. 8 CFR §204.6(j).
257. 8 U.S.C. §1186b.

U.S.[258] In order to remove conditional status, the investor must maintain the investment commitment that formed the basis for her or his admission: there must be evidence that the commercial enterprise is viable at the end of the two-year period.[259] No waiver is available from this requirement, and it does not matter whether the enterprise fails through no fault of the noncitizen investor. Moreover, termination of status is possible within two years if USCIS determines that the terms of the original investor visa have not been met.

346. Petitioners of an employment-based preference may appeal a denial of their petition to the USCIS.

§3. Conditions for Special Categories of Workers

347. Certain nonimmigrants, parolees, asylees, persons granted temporary protection status and other noncitizens who may be eligible to receive work authorization must petition USCIS for employment authorization.[260] Applicants who are authorized to work, under the INA and the regulations, must file a Form I-765 and pay the corresponding application fee, with the director having jurisdiction over the applicant's residence, or the director having jurisdiction over the port of entry at which the noncitizen applies, or an entity designated by USCIS. If denied, there is no right to an administrative appeal. Currently, the fee for applications for employment authorization is USD 380 with the possibility of a fee waiver under certain circumstances.

258. 8 CFR §216.1.
259. 8 U.S.C. §1186a.
260. 8 CFR §274a.12 (2008).

Chapter 3. Sanctions Against Irregular Participation in the Labor Market

§1. Sanctions Against Employers

348. Employers who employ unauthorized workers in the U.S. face civil and criminal sanctions.[261] IRCA made it unlawful for a person or other entity to hire, recruit or refer for a fee, for employment in the U.S., or to continue employment of a noncitizen knowing that the noncitizen is an unauthorized noncitizen. An unauthorized noncitizen is defined as a noncitizen who is not an LPR or authorized to be so employed by the INA or (now) USCIS.[262]

349. In addition, it is unlawful for a person to hire for employment an individual without complying with the employer verification requirements provided in IRCA.

350. IRCA requires employers to verify that an individual is authorized to work in the U.S. by examining a number of specified documents to establish the individual's identity and work authorization. Employers are required to attest, under penalty of perjury, that they have verified that the individual is not an unauthorized noncitizen. The individual worker as well is required to attest that she or he is a USC, a national, an LPR, or a noncitizen authorized to work. Employers and employees must complete Form I-9, Employment Eligibility Verification. Employers are required to keep Form I-9 and make it available for inspection for subsequent review by federal agencies. Form M-274 issued by USCIS is a Handbook for Employers with detailed instructions on the verification of documents and completion of the I-9 Forms.

351. Good-faith compliance with the verification and record-keeping statutory requirements is deemed to be in compliance with the provisions.[263]

352. Employers who are found to have violated the rules on employment of unauthorized workers, however, may be ordered to cease and desist the violation and to pay a civil penalty in an amount determined in part by the number of noncitizens employed and the number of times the employer has violated the rules in the past.[264] In addition, paperwork violations (not involving necessarily the actual employment of unauthorized workers) may result in a civil penalty of not less than USD 100 and not more than USD 1,000 for each individual with respect to whom such violation has occurred.[265] Administrative law judges in an administrative proceeding impose penalties and such orders may be appealed in the federal Court of Appeals for the appropriate circuit for review of the order.

261. 8 U.S.C. §1324a.
262. 8 U.S.C. §1324b(h)(3).
263. 8 U.S.C. §1324a(b)(6).
264. 8 U.S.C. §1324a(e)(4).
265. 8 U.S.C. §1324a(e)(5).

353. Employers who engage in a pattern or practice of violations of the rules on employing unauthorized noncitizens may face criminal charges. The sanctions for a violation of these rules by employers are a fine of not more than USD 3,000 for each unauthorized noncitizen with respect to whom such a violation occurs and imprisonment for not more than six months or both.[266]

§2. Sanctions Against Workers

354. Working without authorization may constitute a violation of the terms of a noncitizen's visa, the conditions upon which they were admitted to the U.S. Violating the terms or conditions of admission renders a noncitizen removable. Thus, for example, a tourist who accepts employment while visiting the U.S. risks being removed because in accepting employment they have violated the terms of her or his visa.

355. Noncitizen workers who enter without inspection or work without documents may be subject to removal because they have entered without inspection and are present in the U.S. without a visa.

356. Noncitizen workers who use fraudulent documents to secure employment face criminal prosecution for document and other fraud. Use of fraudulent documents also renders noncitizens deportable.

266. 8 U.S.C. §1324a(f).

Chapter 4. Legal Remedies and Procedural Safeguards

357. As a general matter, noncitizen workers receive the same level of protection under U.S. employment and labor laws as citizens. As a practical matter, however, noncitizen workers may face difficulties in pursuing remedies when or if they are no longer in the U.S. Unauthorized workers may face additional barriers, as the U.S. Supreme Court held in *Hoffman Plastic Compounds, Inc. v. NLRB*,[267] that in some cases they may not recover financial damages or financial remedies when employers violate the workers' labor rights. To some extent this area of the law is unsettled.

358. In particular, the INA prohibits discrimination based on national origin or citizenship status (other than an unauthorized noncitizen), with respect to the hiring or recruitment of an individual for employment. The prohibition includes terminations from employment. Exempted from the anti-discrimination provisions are employers who employ three or fewer employees; if the discrimination is covered by Title VII; or if the discrimination on the basis of citizenship status is required in order to comply with federal, state or local law.[268] Protected individuals are USCs and U.S. nationals; LPRs and asylees, except for LPRs who become eligible for naturalization and fail to file for naturalization within six months, unless the noncitizen can establish that she or he is actively pursuing naturalization.

359. The anti-discrimination rules allow an employer a preference in hiring for a USC over a noncitizen, in the case of two individuals equally qualified.[269]

360. Individuals must choose between filing under (i) Title VII under the Civil Rights Act of 1964[270] with the Equal Employment Opportunity Commission, or (ii) the IRCA unfair immigration-related employment practice with the Special Counsel for Immigration-Related Unfair Employment Practices. Administrative law judges decide IRCA complaints and employers may be imposed civil penalties including injunctive relief and financial penalties, including back pay. In addition, a prevailing party may recover a reasonable attorney's fee, if the losing party's argument is without reasonable foundation in law and fact. IRCA penalties may be appealed to the Federal Court of Appeal for the circuit in which the violation is alleged to have occurred. Workers discriminated against on the basis of national origin may receive more favorable treatment under Title VII of the Civil Rights Act of 1964, because Title VII allows aggrieved workers to file an action in court with the possibility of more generous remedies.

---

267. 535 U.S. 137 (2002).
268. 8 U.S.C. §1324b.
269. 8 U.S.C. §1324b(a)(4).
270. 42 U.S.C. §§20003 et seq.

Part VIII. Access to Self-Employed Activities

Chapter 1. Overview of Applicable Legislation

361. The INA does not make specific provision for self-employed activities other than through the immigrant employment preference categories already described or the nonimmigrant employment visa categories. The immigrant employment preference that is most analogous to self-employment is the preference of immigrant investors.

Chapter 2. Conditions for Entitlement to Work in the Country as a Self-Employed

§1. General Conditions

362. The employment-based preference for immigrant investors in new commercial enterprises allocates 10,000 visas for the investors, their spouse and children. Immigrant investors do not have to satisfy labor certification requirements. To be eligible for this visa, noncitizens must make a capital investment of at least USD 500,000 in certain "target employment areas" and at least USD 1 million in other "high employment areas."[271] "Targeted employment areas" are rural areas and areas experiencing high unemployment rates. The investment must benefit the economy of the U.S. and must create full-time employment for at least ten qualified employees within two years (or a reasonable time) of admission.[272] Qualified employees include USCs, LPRs, asylees, refugees and other noncitizens. The immigrant investor, her or his immediate relatives, and nonimmigrants are not counted toward the "qualified employees" for the purpose of this visa.[273]

363. The law requires that the investor be engaged in the management of the enterprise. This requirement may be met by holding a seat on the board of directors of the enterprise.[274]

§2. Administrative Rules and Procedures

364. Noncitizens applying for an employment-based investor visa must file a petition on Form I-526. The petition must be submitted with evidence that the commercial enterprise has been established; that the petitioner has invested in the enterprise; that the capital used to invest was acquired lawfully; that the commercial enterprise has created, or will create, at least ten full-time positions for qualified employees; that the petitioner is an active investor and that she or he will be involved in the management of the enterprise; if the enterprise is in a targeted area, proof that the area satisfies the requirements of a targeted area, and any other evidence deemed necessary to process the application.[275]

365. Noncitizens admitted as immigrant investors, and their spouse and children are admitted conditionally for two years and must petition for the removal of conditional status within ninety days immediately preceding the second anniversary of the noncitizen having been granted such status.[276] Failure to apply for removal of the conditional status will result in automatic termination of lawful status in the

271. 8 CFR §204.6(f).
272. 8 U.S.C. §1153(a)(5)(A)–(C).
273. 8 CFR §204.6(f).
274. 8 CFR §204.6(j)(5).
275. 8 CFR §204.6(j).
276. 8 U.S.C. §1186b.

U.S.[277] In order to remove conditional status, the investor must maintain the investment commitment that formed the basis for her or his admission: there must be evidence that the commercial enterprise is viable at the end of the two-year period.[278] No waiver is available from this requirement and it does not matter whether the enterprise fails through no fault of the noncitizen investor. Moreover, termination of status is possible within two years if USCIS determines that the terms of the original investor visa have not been met.

§3. Conditions for Special Categories of Self-Employed

366. There are no other immigrant admission categories for self-employment.

277. 8 CFR §216.1.
278. 8 U.S.C. §1186a.

Chapter 3. Sanctions Against Irregular Exercise of Self-Employment

367. There are no special sanctions targeting irregular exercise of self-employment other than the civil and criminal sanctions already described against unauthorized employment of noncitizens. Immigrant investors who fail to remove conditional status are entitled to a removal hearing, as are all other immigrant categories.

Chapter 4. Legal Remedies and Procedural Safeguards

368. The legal remedies and procedural safeguards for noncitizens who work in the country as self-employed are the same as for other immigrants and nonimmigrants. Immigrant investors who fail to remove conditional status are entitled to a removal hearing prior to deportation.

Selected Bibliography

Aleinikoff, Martin & Motomura, Fullerton. *Immigration and Citizenship*. 6th ed. St. Paul, Minnesota: West, 2008.

Aleinikoff, T. Alexander & Chetail, Vincent. *Migration and International Legal Norms*. The Hague, The Netherlands: T.M.C. Asser Press, 2003.

Bodnar, John. *The Transplanted: A History of Immigrants in Urban America*. Bloomington, Indiana: Indiana University Press, 1985.

Daniels, Roger. *Japanese Americans, from Relocation to Redress*. Salt Lake City, Utah: University of Utah Press, 1986.

Fragomen, Austin T. Jr. & Bell, Steven C. *Immigration Fundamentals: A Guide to Law and Practice*. 4th ed. New York, New York: Practicing Law Institute, 2008.

Griswold del Castillo, Richard. *The Treaty of Guadalupe Hidalgo: A Legacy of Conflict*. Norman, Oklahoma: University of Oklahoma Press, 1990.

Handlin, Oscar. *The Uprooted*. Philadelphia, Pennsylvania: Little, Brown, 1952.

Hutchinson, Edward P. *Legislative History of American Immigration Policy 1798–1965*. Philadelphia, Philadelphia: University of Pennsylvania Press, 1981.

Irons, Peter H. *Justice at War*. New York, New York: Oxford University Press, 1983.

Johnson, Kevin. *The "Huddled Masses" Myth: Immigration and Civil Rights*. Philadelphia: Temple University Press, 2004.

Johnson, Kevin. *How Did You Get to Be Mexican?: A White/Brown Man's Search for Identity*. Philadelphia: Temple University Press, 1999.

Johnson, Kevin & Bernard Trujillo. *Immigration Law and the U.S.-Mexico Border: Si se puede?* Tucson: University of Arizona Press, 2011.

Kurzban, Ira J. *Immigration Law Sourcebook*. 11th ed. Washington, D.C.: American Immigration Law Foundation, 2008.

Legomsky, Stephen H. & Rodriguez, Cristina. *Immigration and Refugee Law and Policy*. 5th ed. New York, New York: Foundation Press, 2009.

Miller, Stuart C. *The Unwelcome Immigrant: The American Image of the Chinese, 1785–1882*. California: University of California Press, 1969.

Motomura, Hiroshi. *Americans in Waiting: The Lost Story of Immigration and Citizenship in the United States*. Oxford; New York: Oxford University Press, Inc., 2006.

Ngai, Mae M. *Impossible Subjects: Illegal Aliens and the Making of Modern America*. Princeton, New Jersey: Princeton University Press, 2004.

Neuman, Gerald L. *Strangers to the Constitution: Immigrants, Borders, and Fundamental Law*. Princeton, New Jersey: Princeton University Press, 1996.

Ross, William G. *Forging New Freedoms: Nativism, Education, and the Constitution, 1917–1927.* Nebraska: University of Nebraska Press, 1994.
Salyer, Lucy E. *Laws Harsh as Tigers: Chinese Immigrants and the Shaping of Modern Immigration Law.* Chapel Hill, North Carolina: University of North Carolina Press, 1995.
Weber, David J. *Foreigners in Their Native Land: Historical Roots of the Mexican Americans.* Albuquerque, New Mexico: University of New Mexico Press, 1996.
Weber, David J. *The Mexican Frontier 1821–1846: The American Southwest under Mexico.* Albuquerque, New Mexico: University of New Mexico Press, 1982.
Weber, David J. *The Spanish Frontier in North America.* New Haven, Connecticut: Yale University Press, 1992.
Wunder, John R. (ed.). *Law and the Great Plains: Essays on the Legal History of the Heartland.* Westport, Connecticut: Greenwood Press, 1996.
2005 Yearbook of Immigration Statistics, Office of Immigration Statistics, Department of Homeland Security (2006).

Government Web Sources

Office of Immigration Statistics, Department of Homeland Security, *Immigration Statistics*, available at http://www.dhs.gov/office-immigration-statistics.
U.S. Census Bureau, U.S. Department of Commerce, available at www.census.gov/.
U.S. Citizenship and Immigration Services, Department of Homeland Security, available at www.uscis.gov/portal/site/uscis.
U.S. Immigration and Customs Enforcement, Department of Homeland Security, available at www.ice.gov/.
U.S. Customs and Border Protection, Department of Homeland Security, available at www.cbp.gov/.
U.S. Department of State available at www.state.gov.
U.S. Department of Justice, Executive Office for Immigration Review available at www.usdoj.gov/eoir.

United States Statutes and Regulations

Title 8, United States Code, as amended.
Chapter 8, United States Code of Federal Register (2013).

Index

The numbers here refer to paragraph numbers.

Admission, 31, 32, 33–37, 46, 51, 53, 58, 62, 63, 67, 80, 98, 99, 101, 105–109, 112–115, 117, 119, 120, 122–124, 126, 135, 137, 141, 144–159, 162, 171, 173, 175, 177, 185, 198, 202, 210, 212–224, 228, 235–238, 242, 247, 265, 272, 273, 283, 287, 299, 319, 324, 325, 327, 334, 340–345, 354, 362, 365, 366
Appellate review, 96, 119, 170, 217, 219, 225, 231, 299, 300, 304, 306–309, 346, 352
Asylum, 63, 71, 79, 81, 94, 96, 99, 201, 204, 210–227, 239, 273, 274, 283, 287, 301, 309, 322

Board of Immigration Appeals (BIA), 34, 64, 96, 213, 225, 286, 301, 304, 321, 322

Cancellation of removal, 239, 249, 262, 305, 306, 310, 314
Chinese Exclusion Acts, 51
Convention against torture, 83, 224–226

Department of Homeland Security (DHS), 42, 43, 44, 48, 54, 73, 76, 78, 81, 91–93, 96, 110, 120, 147, 179, 180, 187, 203, 220, 222, 223, 247, 284, 315, 317
Department of Justice (DOJ), 54, 72, 79, 91, 96
Department of Labor (DOL), 52–54, 97, 140, 191, 194, 336, 337, 341, 342
Department of State (DOS), 53, 91, 95, 99, 109, 132, 160, 165, 166, 185, 186, 219, 343
Deportation grounds
  aggravated felony, 238, 239, 313
  crimes of violence, 240
  criminal conduct, 237, 239
  entry without inspection, 247, 284
  immigration violations, 235, 258, 263, 305
  national security, 245, 257, 269, 274, 313
  terrorism, 64, 69, 257, 274
DHS. *See* Department of Homeland Security (DHS)
Diversity immigrants, 67, 143, 228, 229
Document fraud, 244, 269, 312, 313
DOJ. *See* Department of Justice (DOJ)
DOL. *See* Department of Labor (DOL)
Domestic violence, 67, 68, 72, 79, 124, 149, 220, 243
DOS. *See* Department of State (DOS)
Drug trafficking, 118
Due process, 14, 24, 81, 171–173, 231, 258, 323

Employer sanctions, 348–353
Employment authorization, 208, 209, 222, 324, 326, 347
Employment preferences, 339, 361
Entry, 40, 50–52, 55, 69, 71, 92, 99, 100, 105–110, 112–127, 131, 134, 161, 191, 194, 201, 217, 235, 246, 247, 260, 264, 267, 284, 289, 291, 322, 332, 347
Entry without inspection, 247, 284
EOIR. *See* Executive Office for Immigration Review (EOIR)

Index

Equal protection, 14, 26, 171, 172
Executive Office for Immigration Review (EOIR), 76, 96, 225

Family preferences, 166, 168, 174

Gender discrimination, 87, 89, 172

Homeland Security Act, 64, 76

IMFA. *See* Immigration Marriage Fraud Amendments (IMFA)
Immediate relatives, 28–37, 62, 144–152, 162, 214, 226, 227, 236, 238, 362
Immigrant categories
  diversity, 67, 143, 228–229
  employment, 28–37, 61, 62, 65, 67, 94, 123, 143, 153, 160, 189, 339, 342, 361, 362, 366
  family, 29–, 37, 53, 61, 62, 67, 94, 123, 143, 152, 153, 158, 166, 174
Immigration and Nationality Act (INA), 61, 62, 64, 65, 67, 73, 101, 112, 113, 116, 120–123, 126–128, 143–146, 149, 152, 155, 168, 177, 183, 190, 191, 198, 202, 206, 211, 213, 214, 217, 222, 228, 230–232, 235, 239, 240, 244, 245, 247, 252–255, 257, 270, 271, 274, 279, 280, 282, 283, 300, 306, 308, 309, 311, 321, 327, 331, 347, 348, 358, 361
Immigration courts, 43, 44, 91, 96, 204, 213, 239, 241, 251, 256
Immigration Marriage Fraud Amendments (IMFA), 64, 66–68
Immigration Reform and Control Act (IRCA), 64, 65, 328, 329, 348, 349, 350, 360
INA. *See* Immigration and Nationality Act (INA)
Inadmissibility grounds
  Communist Party membership, 59
  criminal conduct, 112, 123, 274
  national security, 112, 120, 121, 257, 274, 280, 282
  public charge, 112, 123, 202
  public health, 101, 115, 235, 271
  terrorism, 63, 120, 257, 274, 282
IRCA. *See* Immigration Reform and Control Act (IRCA)

Judicial review, 69, 71, 77, 119, 131, 219, 231, 239, 268, 300, 306, 308, 322

Language discrimination, 24, 177, 214

Marriage fraud, 236

NAFTA. *See* North American Free Trade Agreement (NAFTA)
National origin discrimination, 62, 172, 329, 330, 358, 360
National origins, 53, 61, 62
Naturalization, 47, 52, 54, 56, 67, 76, 94, 102, 103, 150, 155, 174, 210, 244, 327, 358
Nonimmigrants
  business, 46, 95, 105, 109, 110, 128, 129, 132
  pleasure, 105, 128, 129, 132, 136, 177
  tourists, 46, 105, 110, 129
  victims of crime, 73
  workers, 46, 104, 190, 325, 347
North American Free Trade Agreement (NAFTA), 87,
North American tribes or tribal groupings, 7

Parole, 73, 113, 124, 257, 274, 302, 326, 347
Permanent residence, 28–37, 69, 94, 97, 126, 128, 143, 148, 150, 208, 209, 212, 228, 324, 327, 331
Priority workers, 331, 342

Race, 14, 25, 49, 61, 62, 83, 172, 212–214, 217, 223, 224, 281, 330
REAL ID Act, 64, 77
Refugee, 4, 21, 28–37, 58, 63, 64, 71, 79, 80, 83, 198, 201, 204, 205, 210–220, 224, 226, 227, 362
Refugee Act, 58, 63, 64, 83, 220
Removal
  detention, 69, 93
  grounds, 237, 239, 247, 252, 268, 276, 282, 284, 285, 312, 319
  process, 41, 69, 230, 231, 318
  relief, 43, 96, 214, 224, 233, 239, 261, 303, 305, 306, 310

Sex discrimination, 26, 62
Statistics, 1–49
Students, 24, 46, 72, 138, 140, 177–188

Temporary protected status (TPS), 55, 67, 201, 222, 223, 226
Terrorism, 21, 64, 69, 74, 75, 76, 92, 120, 257, 274, 282
TPS. *See* Temporary protected status (TPS)
Trafficking, 72, 73, 90, 204, 208, 209, 295–97

Unauthorized immigrants, 40, 41, 112
Unauthorized migration, 48, 71
Undocumented immigrants, 40, 41
Unlawful presence, 202, 207
U.S. Citizenship and Immigration Services (USCIS), 73, 76, 94, 95, 102, 108, 111, 140, 148, 154, 159, 160, 162, 178, 194, 204, 215, 225, 244, 315, 324, 326, 341–348, 350, 365
U.S. Constitution, 1, 2, 14, 48, 50, 121, 169, 172, 173, 231, 296, 323
U.S. Customs and Border Protection, 76, 92
U.S. Immigration and Customs Enforcement (ICE), 43, 44, 45, 76, 93, 201, 204, 216, 250, 255, 274, 286
U.S.-Mexico-Canada Agreement, 87, 133, 176
U.S. Supreme Court, 14, 17, 24–26, 51, 59, 80, 81, 85, 86, 170, 171, 172, 173, 213, 214, 231, 234, 239, 240, 274, 306, 308, 316, 317, 322, 323, 328, 357

Visas
  application, 94, 102, 110, 132, 140, 162, 165, 167, 191, 199, 200, 204, 341
  asylum, 94, 99, 201, 204, 214, 217
  cultural exchange, 136, 185, 186
  diversity, 228
  eligibility, 140
  employment based, 62, 97, 123, 214, 324, 327, 338, 340–344, 346, 362, 364
  family based, 166, 214, 324, 327, 342
  immigrant, 62, 66, 94, 96, 143, 144, 162, 165, 170, 188, 189, 335, 342
  nonimmigrant, 65, 73, 95, 132, 136–140, 142, 167, 188, 190, 208, 235
  student, 138, 140, 179, 180, 182
  tourist, 95, 106, 107, 110, 129, 354
  victims of crime, 73, 201
  witnesses of crime, 238
  worker, 136, 190–192, 194, 195, 337, 338

Work authorization, 73, 94, 214, 222, 226, 305, 328, 347, 350

Index